HOW ~~NOT~~
TO BACKSLIDE
IN 30 DAYS OR LESS

Blanche A. Drayton-Robinson

**How Not to Backslide
In 30 Days or Less
by Blanche A. Drayton-Robinson**

Printed in the United States of America

Published by Lee's Press and Publishing Company, LLC

*A Premiere Self-Publishing
Services Company*

Headshot Photography Credit: Imari Mitchell
@lampproductionsphotography

ISBN: 979-8-9886270-7-4

www.LeesPress.net

Dedication

This book is dedicated and written for the souls to use as a tool for those who desire to grow and live confidently as a child of God with handy and perinate information for everyone who likes to be a witness and loves sharing the Gospel.

"And they overcame him by the blood of the Lamb, and by the word of their testimony; and they loved not their lives unto the death." **Rev. 12:11**

Prologue

So often I've asked God, why do people fall into the same trap, over and over, again and again, after they confess you as Savior? Lord, why do converts rejoice over their deliverance and soon fall back into the very same thing they were happy to be out of? Why do some people run the race of Salvation for a while and give up? Why when trials and tests come don't, they remember what YOU brought them out of?

Why does their faith walk sometimes last for such a short period? Why, why, why? That is the Question.

Introduction

"Return, faithless people; I will cure you of backsliding." -
Jer. 3:22 (NIV)

Dealing with the soul is serious business. After so many years of praying for lost souls, encouraging them in their faith, only to see them repent then go back and repeat the same behavior all over, it became very troubling to me. Just in case you're wondering what behavior I'm referring to, it's Backsliding — and preventing or correcting this behavior is the purpose of this book.

You may ask what is backsliding? Then again, you may already know. But just in case you don't, I will present several meanings in the simplest of terms in the hope of making it very clear to you and avoiding any confusion – both for the churched and the unchurched.

Backsliding is the spiritual separation from God by an individual who once professed obeying and testifying to a spiritual transformation that regenerates the spirit within.

Backsliding is a term used within Christianity to describe a process by which an individual who has converted to Christianity reverts to pre-conversion habits and practices.

Also Backsliding is to "turn back" or "turn away." The express purpose of this book is to be a usable tool in your hands as a new convert or a returning regenerate; to become a weapon to inform, reveal, prepare and equip you to handle the different trials and tests the Lord will allow the enemy, Satan, to bring your way to make you a vessel to give Him glory.

Think about the military: The moment a person enlists, they are immediately assigned to boot camp, a training ground. Why, it's to prepare them for battle against the enemy, to help them survive the attacks of the enemy they will be fighting. Your enemy, the devil, God's diabolical enemy, will come to you, harass you, and annoy you because he (the devil) is no longer in control of you and he's not a happy camper that you left him. Therefore, you need a powerful weapon – this book – for boot camp. The Bible is the Word of God, and this book is in no way to replace it. It's a tool to help you gain strength and see the devil for who he really is, while you study and grow. Boot camp teaches you how to stay alive and help others, as well. This is what this book will do for you: Help you stay alive spiritually and remain focused so you can stay "saved."

I had been bothered for years about souls who confessed Christ as Savior, who last for a while in that commitment, then turn away from Him. They appeared to be glad to be rid of the worldly baggage that had held them captive for many, many years, and decided to surrender to Christ. Many turned to the Lord because they were overwhelmed, burdened and not able to take another step in any direction after trying so many other failed avenues and ventures and attempts to get peace and freedom.

Some suffered from drug abuse, alcoholism, womanizing,

sexual promiscuity and all the usual sins due to the fall of man (Adam) in the Garden of Eden. Which caused every person to be born in sin and shaped in iniquity **(Ps. 51: 5).** Therefore, leaving every person destined to walk after their own lusts **(2 Pet. 3:3).** As my brother, Bishop G. Drayton, would always say, "stinking from drinking, choking from smoking and needing a checkup from the neck up." Words never rang so true. As in **Romans 3:23**: "For we all have sinned and come short of the glory of God." That's why I wondered – knowing the power of God and his saving grace, how can anyone walk away?

This I saw repeatedly. Different individuals, once they accepted Christ, you could see the change in their life, their countenance, brightness and smiles on their faces, their outerwear changed for the better. But after a few weeks, months, or years, they fall back into the same behavior they were happy to be rid of. They seem to take the road less traveled and begin attending churches where anything goes, or they don't go at all. In this area, it's not hard to do.

It was very disturbing to me and still is, to see God pour out His Spirit and blessings when they come to Him, weary, worn, sad, sick or lame. They run like someone is chasing them, they want to testify, and they want to do whatever their hands find fit to do (which is a good thing), no problem there. It's when the first test, trial or opposition comes and they give up, make excuses for why they can't attend church, as if God didn't do anything for them. It made me wonder, "Lord what is wrong; what's missing?" Why would they, from the time they accept you and experience your love, peace and joy as the scripture says, "... Now turn again to the weak and beggarly elements, where unto ye desire again to be in bondage?" **Galatians 4:9**

As a born-again believer in Christ and Intercessor, it bothered me to see Him put back through a senseless death, repeatedly. Please don't get me wrong. I know everyone will not be saved, and that's unfortunate; and I also know that God is not willing that any perish. But I would hope that those who are not saved are those who just flat-out rejected Him, not those who have tasted of his goodness. Oh, I know there are some who believe "once saved always saved." If you believe this, hold that thought, because that's a horse of a different color. Check this out. Is it not true? "Holiness without which no man shall see the Lord. ... ?" **Heb. 12:14.** I say let's strive for perfection, "But put ye on the Lord Jesus Christ, and make no provision for the flesh, to fulfill the lusts thereof." **Rom. 13:14.**

"Who will be saved?" as my mother always said about the gray areas in life. "Only God in heaven knows." That's why I say, as the scripture says: "If you walk in the spirit, you will not fulfill the lust of the flesh" **(Gal. 5:16)** and you will be holy.

When you talk to the backslider, you will get excuse after excuse as to why they can't attend Bible Study and Prayer or Sunday Morning Services. How they have to work, or the kids are involved in this type of sport, and they have this to do and that to do. This type of behavior has been the beginning of backsliding for many. Sometimes, something may have been said or a misunderstanding happens.

Instead of understanding that there's a problem that they need to deal with, they choose to run away – and end up in the very same predicament that brought them to Christ in the first place. Don't run away from Christ. Run to Him in Prayer or to the Pastor, to help you through the difficult time – because troubles or difficulty are going to always be there. You will have trouble, period. That's life! But Jesus is a friend who sticks closer than a brother or sister.

"Man, that is born of a woman is of few days, and full of trouble. **Job 14:1**

"Good people suffer many troubles, but the Lord saves them from them all." **Ps. 34:19 (GNB)**

Here's something I pray you and every individual gets to know: When you decide to follow Christ, there are always going to be some great challenges, great challenges. The scriptures are loaded with individuals who faced extreme persecution; and just like everything else in life, there are always new undertakings and oppositions. For example, a new job, marriage, becoming a new mother or father, learning to drive, moving into a new neighborhood, going to a new school or college, buying a new home, taking exams for a promotion, raising children or renting – the list is endless; but your ability to make adjustments is second to none because God has given man that type of ability to reason, to figure things out. God has equipped humankind with the ability to cope because he has promised to help us.

As a new believer, it's important to know God will strengthen, as his word says in, **Phil. 4:13,** "I can do all things through Christ who strengthens me." Your innate ability takes over, powered by the Word of God within your spirit. If you want it badly enough, you will handle it by taking hold of the Word. Salvation is no different. One must always understand that a desire is only achieved, always, when it is based on how badly you want it. Salvation carries the same principle.

Salvation (to be rescued from the destruction to come) is a must for every person if you want to escape the destruction that's going to come upon this earth. The choice is yours, but it's left up to you and every individual to make up their own mind if this is what they want. You must be determined within yourselves if it's worth it to go through the struggles or not. Because if salvation doesn't mean much, if it's not valuable to you, you will not guard it with every ounce of faith and determination you can muster up. As in everything, you must always take inventory in every challenge you face. When opposition comes, you must consider and ask yourself questions such as, "Why am I being hassled?" "Why is it so difficult after accepting Christ?" "Why is it trying to be taken away from me?" To research, question and observe any situation is a very good place to start. First question: What is the value of your possession? Think about what thieves do to get diamonds, well-known art pieces, gold (think of the Gold Rush) and anything deemed worthwhile. Your quest for God must be understood with sincere and genuine knowledge that God is real and his word is truth. "... for he that cometh to God must believe that he is and that he is a rewarder of them that diligently seek him." **(Heb. 11: 6)**. Understanding these three things is a great place to start.

1. Come to God, believe that He is.
2. Believe that He is a rewarder.
3. Believe He will be found by those who diligently seek him.

Everything that's built must start with a solid foundation if you want it to last. Every person who wants to develop a strong, lasting and stable foundation has to start by getting to know Jesus. He is the solid foundation on which to build a spiritual relationship that will last through hard times, dark times, and any trying times that He will allow to come your way. Yes, God allows every difficulty you encounter. Each challenge will bring you to a point of understanding; you must decide whether you are going to trust Him or return to what you know. When those unstable situations arise, they come to strengthen you. How does it strengthen you? You must decide to do that which is right according to God's Word, not what makes you feel comfortable or self-satisfied or justified. Let me share with you one of the many challenges I have faced.

I am a teacher by profession. One day as I was walking down the hallway of the school where I was teaching, one of the aides came walking towards me. As she came close to me, she swung her shoulder very swiftly in order to hit my shoulder. She did it very forcibly; had she succeeded in hitting me, it would have caused me to hurt, badly. But very smoothly, God allowed me to move out of the way, and what she was trying to accomplish was unsuccessful. This went on for several days. In the meantime, I'm trying to figure out what's gotten into her that she wanted to pick a fight with me. Well, I asked, "What devil has gotten into her?" Even my teacher's aide saw her in action one day and said to me, "She just tried to hit you." I said to her, "Yeah, I don't know what her problem is." After a while, enough was enough. I became very annoyed, and while in the restroom one day, in my frustration, I told the Lord: "I have had enough. The next time she tries to bump into me, it is on." I had made up in my mind I was going to snatch her so fast and slam her into the locker so hard, she wouldn't know what happened. But then, the Word of God came to me as clear as a light being turned on in a darkroom. "Vengeance is mine." **(Rom. 12:19).** Well, needless to say, my plan to fight back was put to rest. Trusting God is more than just talk. It's like this: "If you gonna talk the talk, you gotta walk the walk."

Acknowledgements

This has been a long journey getting this book into print once again. I've learned nothing good comes easy, and this journey proved so. Getting to this point was met with a few challenges, but thanks to my daughter, Cookie, and her skills, including resilience and perseverance, got me to this god-appointed time. I'm eternally and forever grateful for being a vessel for the God who spoke this World into existence.

To my Editor, Karen Keefe, kudos to you. You reassured me the material compiled would benefit everyone, whether they are Bible students or not, and also to my publisher, Lee's Press and Publishing Company for your expertise.

To my dear loving husband, I honestly do thank God for you. I love you. I'm thankful for your patience and for giving me the space to be used by God for this assignment. When you informed me that you were reading my book for the second time, it was uplifting and overwhelmingly validating. Thank you for being you.

"To open their eyes, and to turn them from darkness to light, and from power of Satan unto God, that they may receive forgiveness of sins, and inheritance among them which are sanctified by faith that is in me." **Acts 26:18**

CHAPTER 1

WEEK ONE:

Counting the Cost – Christ as Your Buffer

*"For which of you, intending to build a tower, sitteth down first and counteth the cost, whether he have sufficient to finish it." - **Luke 14:28***

DAY 1: Realize the value of salvation and the price Jesus paid for your sins.

DAY 2: Learn what to do when the Honeymoon is over, and the devil tests you.

DAY 3: Study the Word.

DAY 4: Know how much Jesus loves you.

DAY 5: Call on Jesus as your foundation to face the tests.

DAY 6: Seek guidance from God and the Holy Spirit.

DAY 7: Pray, spend time talking to God and walk with the Lord.

The Value of Salvation

My husband had decided that every year, we would go on a trip to have quality time as a family and to expose our children to different cities and people and how they live and the jobs that they do; also, to have memories as a family. He worked out our budget every year in order that there would be money available when the time came to go. Therefore, we'd have what we needed. When we left, he was very meticulous about securing our home to make sure no one was at liberty to just walk in and take out what they figure they wanted to take. We may not have had in our possession extremely expensive paintings or gold-plated dishware, but what we had was ours; we bought it with our hard-earned cash, and it was valuable to us. So, with that in mind, every necessary precaution was taken to secure our valuables. Everything had to be calculated financially and steps checked out to ensure our opportunity to take our trip.

When it comes to your salvation, the same concerns and precautions must be taken and considered. Here is the problem: If you don't learn and appreciate what Christ did for you, the World and me through the agony, shame and excruciating pain He suffered on the cross of Calvary, you will not guard your salvation like you guard your own valuables. But when you understand through close fellowship and relationship with Him, you will comprehend and sincerely appreciate the price He (Jesus) paid. You must, every day, do daily maintenance (if I may use this terminology; in our case, knowing how much money we had to save per pay period) spiritually; understand what it takes, how you should and must calculate and tabulate the cost to maintain each and every day (if it means making sacrifices). How important it is for you to make Bible Study (putting money in the bank for future use). Why you should study (to know where you're going and what it takes to get there). Why you should invest in your church (in you and your family). Why you should be accountable to your leaders (direction). Why you should pray as Jesus instructed you to pray (staying on course). The list goes on and on. If you fail to understand the value (family, God's Word) you will not value (secure it), and the thief will take it away. That is precisely the very thing he wants to do.

When the Honeymoon is Over

When you first give your life to Christ, what is new and wonderful is the joy you feel, the elation that keeps you coming for what I will call the "honeymoon" period (you love everybody, and everything is going extremely well). You love being around the saints, you love the songs of praise, studying the Word, etc. If you don't take the necessary steps in maintaining or staying connected to the fellowship of the saints, then the enemy will succeed in his mission to take away the love and joy you first experience during your "Honeymoon" period. You will become cold and indifferent, longing for the familiarity of your old life. What's your cost? What do you have to pay? Jesus paid the full cost for the sins of humankind. The believer's cost is really nothing. All you or any person has to do is to totally come to God through

His Son, Jesus Christ, and accept the responsibility to read the fine print (the Word), the "Will," the God-anointed record.

It's simple but serious.

For this reason, Christ is the mediator of a new covenant, that those who are called may receive the promised eternal inheritance—now that he has died as a ransom to set them free from the sin committed under the first covenant.

In the case of a will, it is necessary to prove the death of the one who made it, because a will is in force only when somebody has died; it never takes effect while the one who made it is living. **Heb. 9:15-17 NIV**

Study the Word

The Holy Ghost – or as some call Him, the Holy Spirit – is still one in the same person. He is the chosen one to help you understand what was written through a Spirit-full-Leader. You can't just read the fine print; you've got to study and pray for understanding. Paul wrote to Timothy concerning the very same matter in **2 Tim. 2:15**, study… The biggest enemy of this world is the biggest enemy of God. He's the devil, himself. The moment you take a true step of faith towards God by accepting Jesus Christ as your Savior, you will find out that you've enlisted in the biggest fight of your life. Satan, in himself, feels he owns you and will not accept your leaving him for another. You must understand and realize that he is real, and he is a jealous lover. He will harass, stalk, aggravate and agitate you in every possible way he can to get you to return to him. The more you refuse, the more he heightens his tactics of fear, loneliness, lack or worldly goods. When that doesn't work, he tries death threats, from serious illnesses to bodily harm. He's making you think he is going to kill you, or you are going to die. That's why it is so very important for you to understand and know that God is very much aware of the devil's tactics and what he's doing to you. He will protect you. God allows these situations to happen because they are for your learning to trust Him and to get to know Him personally. I will repeat this many times because it's true and it bears repeating: God allows these things because he wants his children to grow, and in your growing, you will learn that he is faithful.

I can recall the days of my infancy of salvation, with two young active boys settling them down at night for bedtime, reading them stories, praying with them, taking last-minute requests for milk, juice, Kool-Aid (one of their favorites) or cookies — just mommy time, then kisses and good nights. I would leave their room to go clean up. After a few minutes, I would check on them, and they would be out cold, sound asleep. That's when I would make myself comfortable after cleaning up. While waiting for my husband to come home, I'd get my Bible and sit to study the Word. That's when it was so quiet you could hear a pin drop. As soon as I started reading, all of a sudden one of them would scream like someone had stuck them with a pin. This happened for about two nights. The night I realized where that was coming from, I went into the room, and I began to pray and rebuke the devil. I didn't have that problem any more after that prayer. My sons slept like babies. I had to pray to get them up in the mornings (Not really).

God permits the devil to try his children simply because He wants to give you a testimony (your personal experience), your evidence of your connection to the God you sing and shout about. He's able to brag on you in the face of the devil or simply to those who don't believe, like a natural parent to their child. Remember, it's only a test. Just study the Word and surround yourself with people who pray and study God's Word and have been tried in the fire or have some battle marks (testimonies); you will not have to surrender or retreat. You will pass your test every time. Those whom you surround yourself with will help you to grow in the love of God and wisdom. Have you ever heard the saying, "If you want to know what your future looks like, look at who your friends are"? You will make God proud as any parent would be of a child coming home excited with the news of how they passed their spelling or math test with flying colors. So many will shout and dance over Job's deliverance, but can they "stand" to dance on their own victory?

There are treasures in the Word of God, as well as protection. That's why it's important for you to study. Studying the Word will give you ammunition to fight with and to stay strong, to encourage yourself, as well as others. Scriptures such as:

...When the enemy shall come in like a flood, the spirit of the Lord shall lift up a standard against him. **Is. 59:19**

God is our refuge and strength, a very present help in trouble. **Ps. 46:1**

... lo, I am with you always, even unto the end of the world. **Matt. 28:20**

Casting all your care upon him; for he careth for you. **1 Pet. 5:7**

I can do all things through Christ which strengthened me. **Phil. 4:13**

But my God shall supply all your need according to his riches in glory by Christ Jesus. **Phil. 4:19**

And we know that all things work together for good to them that love God, to them who are the called according to his purpose. **Rom. 8:28**

Being confident of this very thing, that he which hath begun a good work in you will perform it until the day of Jesus Christ: **Phil 1:6**

God has given promises throughout His Word. Nothing in this world can or will be able to destroy it or change it. Your faith will increase through the studying of God's word and fellowship. When you understand during the trials and tests you face, it will cause you to trust Him, knowing He will bring you through. God's Word is the weapon you will need to defeat the devil or any temptations. Matthew, Chapter 4, gives a very good example of how the devil must be dealt with. Also understand that you do not have to go it alone: There will be people to help you, as well as the Holy Spirit. With help, you will recognize and know that you are able to stand firmly, as the scripture says, "...when the enemy comes in, like a flood the spirit of the Lord will lift up a standard for you against him." **Is. 59:19b**. Just remember, the devil can't kill you. He didn't give you life and he can't take it. You are under the blood of Jesus, therefore you are in "protective custody." What the devil tries to do is entice you to walk away from the things of God, His presence.

"He that dwelleth in the secret place of the most high shall abide under the shadow of the Almighty." **Ps. 91:1**

Know How Much Jesus Loves You

Through fellowship and studying of God's Word, I sincerely understood and realized how much Jesus loved me, and the price he paid for me; I fell in love with Him even more. The more I read and studied His Word, the more I fell in love with Him. I can promise you the same thing will happen in your fellowship. With Jesus, every day is sweeter than the day before, as long as you continue to seek Him daily. I kid you not, there will be difficult days. But every day with Jesus truly is sweeter than the day before, only if you seek Him daily. Jesus' love made me thirst and hunger for Him. After speaking to Him, I finally heard Him speak to me; you will too. Especially hearing Him speak the words "I love you," as he did, only sanctioned within me a deeper thirst and hunger that nothing, anyone could satisfy, take away or quench. Having to trust God starts the moment you accept Jesus as Savior, because it takes faith, and faith is to trust. Then it's done little by little as you fellowship and study His Word.

Now, at this point in my life, I had only my sons. They were young when I graduated from college with my Bachelor of

Science Degree in Elementary and Special Education. I wanted very badly to start teaching right away. My husband was working, and we were doing okay. From the time I was young, I looked forward to graduating with my degree so that I could fulfill my lifelong dream (from the age of 6 years old) to TEACH! I couldn't wait. I had my papers intact and I was ready to change the world with my ability to teach. Every time I heard of an opening; I would apply; open doors closed in my face more times than I can remember.

Then one day out of my frustration and not knowing what else to do I said to the Lord, "Lord you know what I'm best qualified to do. Lord, you place me where you see fit." "In all thy ways acknowledge Him, and he shall direct thy paths." **Prov. 3:6**. One year went by, two years went by and then half a year went by; so, by this time, two and at least a half a year had gone by while I remained at home raising our sons every day and waiting up all times of the night for my husband to come home at midnight.

One Sunday in evening service at my home church, the offering was being taken. A request was made for everyone to give an offering of at least five dollars (Guess what? That was all I had). I said to the Lord, "Lord should I give my last five?" Immediately someone began to sing the song, "Give, Give, Give It in Jesus' Name." It came back to me something my Pastor said in one of the services: "If God speaks once, he will speak again." Of course, I said, "Lord, speak again." Before I could say anything, some way, somehow, in the process I looked down, my Bible was open and in red letters in the book of **Acts 20:35b**, Jesus said: "It is more blessed to give than to receive." Once again, it was a done deal. That was Sunday. Monday morning, I was called to come to City Hall for an interview and sent on a second and didn't have to look for another job. I was hired by the Buffalo Board of Education, and I taught in the system until retirement.

Don't allow the devil to entrap you in negative conversations, thoughts, behavior, speech or anything that demeans nor let him devalue what the Word says. The devil is very cunning (**Gen. 3:1**: "...more subtle than any beast ...") and will attack from any and every angle he possibly can. He will try to make you think that there's something wrong with you as you wait for the move of God to happen in your Life. You are who God made you to be and because you made the choice to follow Christ, you will not lose anything, no matter what thoughts come to your mind. Whoever doesn't like your choice to trust God or appreciate the God in you, well, they have the problem – not you. Your only responsibility is to pray for them. Pray that God opens their eyes, spiritually, that they will focus on Him and accept Him as their personal Savior and Lord, so they can see what God has for them, as well.

Salvation is the primary goal. If you find yourself confused, talk with your pastor and let him or her help you understand the battle you're in. Every church has or should have a system in place to help new converts or returning converts be able to deal with and overcome the trials and tests that are sure to happen. In other words, you will be given training that will support you through your crisis with prayer while you grow and learn to trust God on your own. It's up to every individual to do everything it takes to grow and mature into the beautiful child of God that He birthed them to be. "Let your conversation be without covetousness; and be content with such things as ye have for he hath said, I will never leave thee, nor forsake thee." **Heb. 13: 5**

You must:

- Study the Word (take time to get an understanding of what the Word says about you and what it can do for you. Let it take its place in you, or the devil will take the place). The Psalmist says in **Psalm 119:11** "Thy word have I hid in my heart. That I might not sin against thee."

- Pray (spend time talking with God so that you may get to know Him. You will learn to identify His voice when he talks to you. Knowing His word helps make His voice clear).

- Find support Remember to surround yourself with people who exercise faith in God (I can't stress this enough), who truly trust God and live the same life away from church as they profess in church.

Trials and tests will come – this is what I will call the "Proving Stage." God allows trials and tests to come your way in order for you to be strengthened. Then you will be able to prove what is good, and acceptable, and perfect will of God **(Rom. 12:2b).** In other words, He allows the devil to buffer you. This is when you get to know the real you. What you will be able to do. What you will stand for and won't. Where you are weak or what are your weaknesses. What you are capable of. Only He knows what's in you and has the plan to bring it out of you to replace it with greatness.

A buffer, as Webster's dictionary defines it:

1. Any of various devices or pieces of material for reducing shock or damage due to contact.

2. A means, or device used in a cushion against the shock of fluctuations in business or financial activity; something that serves as a protective barrier: as a Buffer State b: a person who shields another esp. from annoying routine matters c: Mediator.

Let's look at the first meaning. When you enlist into this battle (salvation, the army of God) it isn't about you anymore. It's about God and what He wants to do through you and for you. Therefore, God lets the devil work for Him to make you become your best self. In studying, you will realize and know that in this battle you will decide to stand against the prevailing and popular forms of the spirit of the world and proclaim the eternal truths and righteous standards of God's Word for Christ's sake.

When you embrace the training by enduring and looking at the situations that enter your life as a child of God, you will become empowered. You will be that soldier the Apostle Paul wrote to Timothy about becoming in **2 Timothy 2:3.** When you are put under pressure, it cleans and polishes you to shine like the light God predestined you to become or the finest of gold. God will continue on a daily basis to use you to win souls for His kingdom and defeat the enemy of this world. I did mention "daily." This thought, alone, should

recall too much more as to the nature of our conversation, but I do know it was intense, because I remember how I felt when the Spirit spoke to me as we approached the intersection. He said, "Teach him how to cross the street." I processed very quickly that it was the Lord who had spoken to me; it was right then that I had to teach my son how to cross the street. It was a weird corner because it was a "Y" corner. Cars approached from three different directions. I said to him, "Jamal, when you have to cross the street, you must look all ways to make sure there are no cars coming from any of these directions. When you are sure there are no cars coming, you run as fast as you can across the street." Well, little did I know how soon I would hear those words come back to me!

It was the very next day in the afternoon when I heard a knock at the door. I opened it, and there he was standing there. In my surprise, I asked, "Jamal, how did you get here?" He said, "I walked." I said, "Who helped you cross the street?" He said, "No one. I looked to make sure there were no cars coming and I ran fast across the street." He repeated back to me the very words I had said to him, what the Spirit had instructed me to do. His words were the very same ones I had said to him. This is just an example of the reality of God and how He will lead and guide you. It can be for your own protection or someone else's.

Trials and Tests

Testing times will come, and this will give you the opportunity to show yourself worthy or capable to be called a child of

God. You will find out if you really have "counted up the cost." He did not make a mistake in choosing you. Not that God makes mistakes, but we have the tendency to think He does or make it look as though he does. God wants you to know Him and He wants to prepare you for your destiny by fulfilling your purpose! God's enemy is now your enemy. He will stop at nothing to get you back. You must be determined with a sold-out heart for Christ that the enemy doesn't get you to turn back (backslide). I believe this bears repeating: He will stop at nothing to get you to turn back, so beware!

Here's what God said to the Israelites and is saying to you today:

"And thou shall remember all the way which the Lord thy God led thee forty years in the wilderness, to humble thee, and to prove thee, to know what was in thine heart, whether thou wouldest keep his commandments, or no. And he humbled thee, and suffered thee to hunger, and fed thee with manna, which thou knewest not, neither did thy fathers know ... that man doth not live by bread only, but by every word that proceedeth out of the mouth of the Lord doth man live." **Deut. 8:2-3**

Your trials and tests are designed with you in mind. God has specific plans for you. He has to prepare you for it. In preparation, as the scripture above states, He wants to show you what's in your heart. He wants to show you who you really are. You may have heard the saying, "Talk is cheap." As human beings, we all have the mentality that lets us think we are capable of doing more than we really can.

As a good parent will not just give their child or children things without determining whether or not they can handle it or whether they are ready for it; neither will God bring you out of the world of your surroundings and lavish you with things that you are not ready for. God is more concerned about your soul and that you be saved. Your soul has to be stripped of the things and cares of the world that will inhibit you to the point where you seek things more than you seek Him. God promises to bless you. He says in His Word, "I would that you prosper and be in good health even as your soul prospers." 3 John 2. He knows when you are mature, when you have wisdom that you can handle His Word and THINGS. If you think you can't handle situations, just trust God and see what He does to lead and guide you into all truths. You will learn as you walk with the Lord, you will learn your tests and trials will teach you things about yourself, and how strong your faith in God is. You will be surprised how God works things out for you and how your love for Him will grow and grow, more and more. "If ye then, being evil, know how to give good gifts unto your children, how much more shall your father which is in heaven give good things to them that ask him?" **Matt. 7:11.**

CHAPTER 2

WEEK TWO:

Where Your Strength Lies

DAY 8: Have faith in the Lord.

DAY 9: Fellowship: Be with believers.

DAY 10: Read the Bible and listen to inspirational music.

DAY 11: Don't give up and backslide when you make mistakes.

DAY 12: Arm yourself with the Word of God.

DAY 13: Beware of unbelieving friends.

DAY 14: Commit to truth and show love.

Prayer, a very familiar word to everyone, I'm sure; but sometimes it's the most unfamiliar action to many. Prayer is very, very, very essential to the child of God. The writer Dr. Luke writes in the gospel of St. Luke, to the Gentiles, in Chapter 18, Verse 1: "...men ought always to pray, and not to faint;" this does not mean, that you should stay on your knees 24-7. What it does mean, if you have truly confessed in your heart Jesus Christ as Lord and Savior, openly confessed it to others, you should know that you are a blood-bought and blood-washed, born-again believer, who needs to develop a spirit (desire) of prayer to pray and not give up (not faint). This is true whether situations are going smoothly or whether they are extremely difficult. In doing so, it will draw you near to God, allowing Him to draw near to you, giving you directions each and every day, which will develop praise and worship in you and reasons to magnify Him out of a pure and sincere heart.

Unanswered Prayers Can Be a Blessing

Your spirit (the part that knows), is aware that He is real; you will want to daily talk about the good as well as the bad – that is, what we consider bad (those things you may have wanted to happen, and they didn't). I'll tell you now that as you grow and mature in Christ, you will thank Him for some of those things He didn't allow to happen. Disappointment can be a good thing because in the long run, if you just hang in there, you will find out how sweet it is. I tell you this from personal experience. Here's what I have said to God so many times: "Lord, I thank you for not answering that prayer I prayed. Lord, thank you for not paying attention to me. Just do what is best for me, because you know I don't know what I'm talking about or what's best." This was after a period of time. The scripture is so true when it says "… All things work together for good…." **Rom. 8:28.**

Letting God guide your footsteps with a mind to do what is right, setting a time in your daily routine, to pray – to really spend time getting to know Him on a personal level – will prove to be your greatest tool in living victoriously.

How to get to know God and remain strengthened:

- His word (studying)
- Pray (for guidance, ideas to enhance the kingdom)
- Surround yourself with others who truly know Him or speak positively.
- Fellowship with the saints (a Bible-teaching, Spirit-filled Church)
- Read approved inspirational books.
- Fast (to refrain from food for a specific purpose, or one you choose from Scripture)
- Listen to inspirational music.

When you grow and mature in the Word, your love for God will sustain you. Then whatever the circumstances that come up in your life and people who are around you, whether they are loved ones or not, you will be able to intercede for yourself and others and not have them pull you away from your Savior. When you have developed an up-close-and-personal relationship, you will always have the mindset to intercede (whether you're alone or with others) anyplace, anywhere — not necessarily always at a place recognized as a prayer-accepted place where you must kneel, but with the mind and spirit that's geared ready to talk to God in any situation at any time in your heart. As the scripture says, if you pray in secret, you will be rewarded openly (paraphrased) Matt. 6:4. If you need to pray and you find that there's a place you can go and have some private time with the Lord, that's a great thing.

Arm Yourself Against the Enemy

Therefore, hold fast to Matthew's account in Chapter 6, Verse 8, "... for your father knoweth what things ye have need of, before ye ask him." Don't ever doubt for a moment that the enemy would tell you, "God doesn't care; you're wasting your time; you've made a big mistake; or you are not ready to make this commitment, you need to enjoy life." Let me just put this out there right now: Satan is a liar and the father of lies. The things he will tell you about God, such as "He doesn't care," are further from the truth than anything can ever be. Satan will say anything and try every trick in the book to persuade you to walk away from God or not get to know Him. If he can't persuade you or trick you (reconnect you with friends you hadn't seen or talked to in months or years), he will resort to what he does best, lying. He is cunning, just as he is described in the book of **Genesis 3:1:** "He's more subtle than any beast." Oh, by the way, everything he does is based on lies. He's a liar and cannot tell the truth — there is no truth in him. That's why he does it best. This was demonstrated in the beginning. I repeat, "Satan is a liar and the father of lies." He will try to deceive by any means necessary. If you don't arm yourself against his attack with the WORD of God and other positive influences, you won't stand a chance.

Haven't you heard? Knowledge is power!

"My people are destroyed for lack of knowledge." **Hosea 4:6**

Satan has no say-so about anything until you give him the opportunity to say something by listening to him. Let me remind you of some things he will say: "You can't go out to bars. You can't have any fun. You will miss out on a whole lot of good stuff," just to mention a few. Therefore, he can't say any more than what you will let him say to you. You mustn't listen to negative thoughts or any non-Biblical words. When you, as a child of God, understand how he operates, you will understand this is not guesswork. The Word also reveals the evil person Satan truly is in John 10:10 and what his mission truly is.

Walk by Faith

You can and must walk by faith, trusting in your personal relationship and believing in the Word. Faith comes by hearing, hearing by the Word of God **(Rom. 10:17)**. The devil convinces those who don't know God (the Word), which doesn't take much because if you are not a child of God, then whose are you? There are only two fathers, God the father of Heaven and the god of this World (where we live and exist). Not knowing God is lack of knowledge. By not getting to know the adversary from hearing and studying the Word, he will control you and discourage contact with other believers. He does this through distractions and isolation, which allows him the greatest opportunity and freedom to feed you foolishness (worldly pleasures), keeping you from knowing the truth so you won't have authority over him. He wants to deceive you into thinking he's powerful and to have authority. The truth is, he's not powerful — you are!

With the proper learning and knowledge, you will know and learn the very thing he tries to keep from you. "Ye are of God, little children, and have overcome them; because greater is he that is in you, than he that is in the world." 1 John 4:4 Therefore, when you are born again or regenerated and you get the Word in you, this knowledge and realization of God brings about confidence, because you have armed yourself — not with physical weapons, but with the Word of GOD. "For the weapons of our warfare are not carnal, but mighty through God to the pulling down of strong holds." **2 Corinth. 10:4.** Some Tricks of Satan's trade These weapons are powerful because they are spiritual, and they come from God. Satan has no other attack than trying to change the Word to bring doubt in your mind. For example, look at what he did in the very beginning. In **Genesis 2:16b**, God said, "Of every tree of the garden thou mayest freely eat." Here's what Satan said: **(Genesis 3:1b):** "Ye shall not eat of every tree of the garden?" Creating doubt, in order to start a dialogue. So, holding a conversation with Satan without being committed to God and His word can prove fatal, or at least result in a total separation from God. Sometimes the results are so devastating, only God can fix it or work it out.

So, the same trickery continues to take place today. Nothing has changed — the same game, different name. Getting a good grip on the Word like the Psalmist says in **Psalm 119:11:** "Thy word have I hid in my heart that I might not sin against thee." As I shared with you earlier about the aide who had a problem with me and decided she was going to handle it physically – if I didn't consult the Lord on my feelings, and had I handled the problem myself, it could have gone a different way. Having been taught at a young age by my parents and then after getting to know God on a personal level through His Word, the Spirit was able to communicate to me to allow God to handle the situation. Now it was not easy to just say, "Okay Lord, you handle it," because I was still learning to trust God. I had a student teacher at the time, and I shared with her my feelings. She pretty much said to me something her parents had taught her (and that I was taught by my parents) on dealing with those who would harm you: "You pray for them and let God work it out or deal with it or handle it." Also, the Word that the Spirit had spoken to me: "Vengeance is mine, I will repay." I just needed to admit my feelings. Another lesson to be learned here, "Godly advice": Know who you are talking and sharing your feelings or issues with.

Your ability to be victorious comes through the power of the Word when you ingest it within your spirit; having a good understanding in how it relates to you and making it a part of your life determines whether or not you will have a positive or negative outcome. When you don't take the Word to be a personal part of your life, it will be easily dismissed. Until you make an investment in something, it's not going to mean very much to you — like your home or your car or business. I'll put it to you this way: What's dear to you, you will keep near (or at least have it secure) and you will take care of it.

Invest time into studying the Word and making it a part of your everyday life.

Don't be Misled!

Beware of friends. Many are guilty of the same permissiveness today that took place in the Garden of Eden with Eve, which is letting friends, or unread or unsaved individuals tell them their opinion or their quote of what they think the Word says, as opposed to studying for themselves and seeking God, letting him reveal his truth and knowledge in their spirit and under Spirit-filled and Spirit-led Leaders. As a child of God, you must always be aware of people, places and things.

In Ephesians, Chapter 6, you will find specific instructions as to what the child of God must do in order to win the battle. But first, the battle in the mind must be dealt with, because that's where it all starts – in the mind. Christ says in **Phil. 2:5** "Let this mind be in you, which was also in Christ Jesus": Christ left a perfect place, to come to not just an imperfect place, but a sin-sick place. He suffered humiliation and, as a servant, became obedient unto death. Question: Can He not expect obedience of his Children? Christ's humility of spirit and mind should and must be in and seen in those who are called by His name.

Here are a few of our spiritual weapons, as referenced in Ephesians:

- Commitment to truth (believe and do what the Word says, which you must study so that you will know what it is you must do).

- Faith (which comes by hearing a Spirit-filled Leader teaching and preaching the word of God and you learning).
- Love (showing others the respect and care you want for yourself with true actions — my definition).

I'll get back to this later. Just to get you started, YOU must put on the whole Armor of God. The moment you trust SALVATION to chance, you will be defeated. The very thing the devil wants to happen is for you to feel and become overwhelmed with defeat. Then it is his opportunity to defeat you. Making you feel you should return to him, the weak and beggarly elements of the world **(Gal.4:9)**. Then he will take you further into sin than you were before. It will be your punishment for leaving him in the first place. Don't you think for a moment he won't make you pay or suffer for leaving him. Hear me when I tell you, he will make you pay BIG TIME! Here on Earth or in Hell.

Mistakes Aren't a Reason to Give Up

The Word tells us that if we come to God, we must first believe that he is God and that he is a rewarder of those who diligently seek him **(Heb. 11:6)**. If you knew enough when things were WRONG to seek God, why then won't you continue to seek Him to keep them going RIGHT, even if you make mistakes or things look like they are not going well. God knows and he will help you deal with it (by human means or by your surroundings). He will speak and you will know when He does. Just know that God is in control and is never out of control. He can work it out, just trust (hold fast to what His Word says) Him to do it. You must realize that everything moves by the power of God. Every child of God must understand that they will make mistakes — it comes with life or the territory. It's just like we don't look for trouble, but trouble happens, and we deal with it.

Starting out, praying may not always be easy for you as a new convert or a returning backslider, but you keep at it, little by little. Just talking to God in the name of Jesus, you'll find yourself moving forward like a locomotive. You know how it is with a train — it starts off very, very slowly, but the engineer just keeps applying pressure to the engine; it gains speed, little by little — and before long, the train is full steam ahead. Nothing can stop it, except when the engineer applies the brakes, and that takes a while before it comes to a halt. You'll be so saturated with the mind to pray; you'll have to pull yourself away from prayer and you would look forward to going to prayer service again and again. Before you come to a halt, it would be time to start up again. It's a continuous process for continuous response.

Here's a thought the Spirit brought to my mind, as it may have come to yours. Now, there are times when there are accidents on the tracks, and it stops the train. Things happen. So, there are times when you won't be able to continue your routine of prayer, but you should remain prayerful. God will show you and cause you to avoid those kinds of atrocities (tricks of the devil). He will make a way for you at some other place and time if you have a set time – and you should. You must not become sidetracked when something causes a disruption in your routine of prayer. Let me remind you to remain prayerful and keep seeking God until He shows you what to do. Sometimes, a work schedule may cause the disruption, or it may be a family emergency, vacation, special event or lifestyles of some sort — anything can bring about an interruption. Don't sweat it, just deal with the situation prayerfully and continue to look forward. Keep telling yourself that it's working together for your good. Not to worry if you get stopped — it's an opportunity to encourage yourself and look for another place to resume your special time with the Lord. As I always tell those I teach: Remember, your life may be the only Bible some people ever read. Therefore, don't allow minor setbacks to make you lose your position or your witness as a child of God. I've learned if you don't pray, you will lose your way or become a casual Christian, where anything goes.

I take prayer very, very seriously, as if you didn't know that by now! So, if this seems extreme, well prayer to me has to be extreme. You may have to go out of your way to make it happen on a consistent basis. Now the previous situation mentioned may be a drop in the bucket compared to some great catastrophes that can happen and can almost derail you, but once again — not to worry, God is there. You get stopped, and it's really a rough situation: God may have given you a directive to avoid the mishap, but you — like me in my early walk and later, too — didn't take heed. Your faith is shaken, or the mistake causes guilt. The enemy really works on you hard, making you feel extremely guilty; but when you have the Word in your heart, the Spirit will bring to your memory or have you read it or God gives a word through someone or some means, somehow you will get it and you can and will recover. For the Word says, "My little children, these things write I unto you, that ye sin not. And if any man sin, we have an advocate with the father, Jesus Christ the righteous." **1 John 2:1**

Ask God for Forgiveness

He will deliver (give you release) when you ask Him to God is a loving father who cares about His children, just like we who are parents care for our own children. He wants His children to be blessed to share in His glorious kingdom, to be a vessel of knowledge, to have the ability to spread and present the Good News of Jesus Christ with others and to help strengthen them, as well. There will be times when you will make mistakes and feel like you have messed up, and the pressure that you feel from that transgression is from the devil. He will try to tell you lies — as he did me and every individual in their spiritual infancy — to keep you feeling guilty and ashamed. Some people are not transparent enough to admit that they made, and probably still make, mistakes; but once again, **1 John 1:9** says, "If we confess our sins, he is faithful and just to forgive us our sins and cleanse us from all unrighteousness." Let the Word, and let God, rid you of the guilt and shame. Let me tell you something that's very true: The moment you ask God for forgiveness, you're forgiven. As **Galatians 5:1** says, "Stand fast therefore in the liberty wherewith Christ hath made us free and be not entangled again in the yoke of bondage."

Forgive Yourself

You may find it hard to forgive yourself, saying, "I should have known better," or asking, "What was I thinking?" God will always be there to comfort and encourage you through, by some means or another. The one thing I believe defeats the child of God is when you repent, yet the thought still lingers. You will think, "Why is this still bothering me? I must not be forgiven." This situation is somewhat similar to when you get a cut: You apply the medicine and the cut is still there; but in time — several applications later — before you know it, it's gone. You can see you are healed. The moment you ask God's forgiveness, it's done. But between yourself and the devil reminding you of your mistake, it just takes longer — and sometimes you just have to continue to apply the Word, but just know it's done. It's the devil – he wants to continue to remind you of your past.

How I got rid of him, one day I saw a T-shirt someone was wearing, and it said, "When the devil reminds you of your past, remind him of his future." That did for me. It was very liberating, to say the least. Praise God! I hope that if you are faced with a similar situation, it can be a liberating experience for you, as well.

Be In it to Win it – Don't Give Up

God delivers. There is no cut-off point where He says, "No more." The same way He delivered you the very first time you came to him, He will do it again, again and again if need be. Always be mindful that in every situation, God will repeat

His love for you as if it were your first offense, not considering the situation that brought you to Him in the beginning. From every test, trial, circumstance you encounter, you should learn the power of God's love and avoid repeating any situation He brought you through and out of. You will always, in between your testimonies, be tried from time to time. You must realize that these situations are your spiritual sharpening tools. That's why they come up. It's a test (there's a lesson to learn in every situation), but whatever else comes up against you, you will learn and know He is more than able to deliver you out of all of them. It's a continual process. Continue to testify, even though at times it may get difficult. Remember, as it is found in **Revelation 12:11** "And they (the ones before us) overcame him (the devil) by the blood of the Lamb (Jesus), and the word of their testimony (trials and tests); and they loved not their lives unto death." You must love God the same way entirely, whether things are good or not so good.

I've seen so many times how individuals return back to their previous lifestyle apart from God because of a boyfriend or girlfriend. The first time the test comes, it's like they say, "Thanks, Jesus, for helping me out of my mess. I'll take it from here. I'll talk to you when I need you again."

'The Shadow of Death'

David wrote in the 23rd Psalm, "...As I walk through the valley of the shadow of death, I will fear no evil." The shadow of death – in other words, there's a figment that appears to be real but it's not – it's there to frighten you or to get your attention to prevent you from continuing your journey. But please note what David says, "... As I walk ..." It's a continual motion; movement leading to the desired goal. From another perspective, keep pressing toward the finish line to successfully complete the test God has designed to establish you in your calling. When you get through the valley (Test, as Pastor Rod Parsley of World Harvest Church always says: That's where your enemy comes to die, not you) there's a great reward waiting for you. Whatever valley the Lord brings you to, He will guide you through (there are challenges getting through, but faith has to be developed); there will always be shadows because your adversary, the devil, is always lurking somewhere near to frighten, entice or create diversions. His goal is to get you to abort the place God wants to bring you to, a place where you will find a greater understanding, a greater joy and strength in the Savior you did not know before.

This is how testimonies come about. David continued to walk because he knew the Shepherd was his guide and protector. Therefore, he simply knew beyond the shadow of a doubt what the enemy was trying to do, and the shadow could not harm him (those things that may not be real or an exaggerated reflection of something that's not really real can't really hurt or harm you). In other words, the enemy shows you things, in hopes it will cause you to fear. Remember it's only a shadow, and shadows can't hurt you or anyone.

Through the Word of God, we find that the enemy is as a roaring lion seeking whom he may devour **(1 Pet. 5:8)**, hoping to get you to become frightened and return to familiar territory (the world). The enemy wants you to be doing what you were comfortable doing and solving things the way you were used to solving them, possibly giving you confidence and instant gratification. But remember what I said earlier — you would pay an awesome price. Some pay it by an early death, homelessness, drug addiction or being in and out of jail — there are a variety of things backsliders end up in, but most importantly, they are out of the presence of God. Don't get me wrong, everyone may not end up in an awful situation, but they will definitely be separated from God, and that's awful enough. The world has a saying: "Don't dance to the music if you can't pay the piper."

Expect the Unexpected

Let me help you (as my goddaughter, Veryl, would say). There's a huge misconception that babes in Christ must be aware of, and that is to think that everything is going to be hunky-dory or smooth sailing all the time or all at once when you give your life to Christ. You will have some very fulfilling experiences in the beginning of your conversion, but challenges are going to come from everywhere. Sometimes it's from people you have forgotten about who just resurface; or sometimes they seem to show up or call after running into someone who knows you. Crazy stuff! All I can say is to expect the unexpected. That's one of the telltale signs that you are on the path to something great – don't be fooled.

Also let me say this: When you first come to the Lord, He does lavish you with things, not things that are over the top, so to speak, but enough to get your attention to let you know it's divine. I have referred to this as the "honeymoon" stage – things you will think about wanting or doing, they happen. Perhaps you venture out into something you longed to do, and you succeed. These are real experiences God gives. Why? you might ask. It's simple. He's making Himself known to you on a personal level, in hopes that you will embrace, trust and take time to get to know Him on an intimate level. Just think about it from a natural perspective. When you meet someone and they prove to you they can make things happen for you; think about it, what do you do? Tell everyone you know and whomever will listen. You brag about what this person did for you and how you just met, how and where you met. God created everything and everybody. Scripture says in Ecclesiastes Chapter 3 there is no new thing under the sun.

As you get to know God and testify of your experiences, He will begin to withhold things a little longer so your trust in Him will grow and you believe in who He is, not so much as to what he can do for you. Let me say it like this: Think on how it is when a parent is teaching their toddler to walk, the parent holds the child's hand, arm, shirt anything to help with their balance. This is done many times until the parent feels the child is strong enough and has the balance to go on their own. The child's hand is let go. This is the test to see if the child can go it alone. God uses somewhat the same method when teaching us to trust Him and walk in faith. God knows when to hold our hand and He knows when to let go. One thing for sure, He will never leave you, just as a parent will not abandon their child.

You Have Been Redeemed

Things will become clearer day by day, little by little, as you continue to walk with God. Just don't abort your walk with Him. You must see your need for God. Christ's death for our Salvation is the ultimate price that was paid for a people that didn't deserve it, but only receive it through God's grace. God doesn't just want to solve the problems you created in your life when you didn't know Him; but also, the ones you will encounter after; He wants to give you experiences to expose the gifts within you to bring out greatness He placed in you. Also understand when you come to know him personally, it goes so much deeper than a simple rescue. It has to do with the internal soul – for the eternal journey, a lost soul on its way to hell. Issues created by one's own hand take time and careful study of God's word for proper guidance to help rid you of them. So many fail to get that info right at the beginning of their conversion. It's not about programs, it's not about entertainment, it's not about joining the right department of the church, the right auxiliary or your talents or your gifts. It is that you were on your way to HELL, and you have been REDEEMED!

Let's talk about the word "redeem" (buy back, repurchase) for a moment. Think about it: "redeem." If you have been "redeemed," you must have been "deemed" – and you were, before Adam disobeyed God. You must understand this very point, which is, because of what happened in the beginning in the Garden of Eden when Adam made the wrong choice, the world was sold out – you and me, along with all the rest of the world. But God had a plan from the beginning to buy us back through the blood of Jesus, who paid the price to redeem, to bring us back, into fellowship with God; for those who accept Him.

Unless you acknowledge Jesus Christ as Lord and Savior, your focus will be on the wrong (worldly) things. Backsliding will slip in so easily; you won't even know you're there until you are. Then it's too late, you're there trying to find a way out. I have seen so many return to their former lifestyle of sin and find themselves into deeper stuff. It has been said, "Sin will take you farther than you want to go or thought you would ever go." But it's never too late to repent as long as you have breath in your body, and you are sincere. Repent with Godly sorrow (when you truly see your transgression and sincerely want to return to God) for your transgression **(2 Cor. 7:10),** it's not too late to return to God, but it must be done with a repentant heart, and you must do your first works over again **(Rev. 2:4-5).**

I cannot reiterate this enough: If you play around with the devil, you will have to play by his rules. He is slick. At first, he lets you think you are getting away with the wrong that you're doing, but the truth of the matter is, you're just getting by. Before you know it, he will have you in so deep that it becomes a life-or-death situation. Through every situation, you have to learn how to trust God, no matter how difficult it gets. The way you learn how to trust God is not any different from what I told you all through this book: Pray, read God's Word and fast (sometimes) and it will help also to get (if you don't already have) a mature, God-fearing believer to pray with you and for you, to talk with you while God is strengthening you, to become the person you were born to become.

I repeat the "old you" must be crucified, and God will allow pressure to do it. When God allows the pressure to find you, it's just washing, cleansing, shaping and establishing you to be able to be His voice, His witness and His example. Don't ever think God doesn't love you when going through your testing period, because He does. He has to prepare you to be the vessel He has ordained for you to be, but the enemy will try to convince you otherwise. "For whom the Lord loveth He chasteneth and scourgeth every son whom He receiveth. If ye endure chastening, God dealeth with you as with sons; for what son is he whom the father chasteneth not? But if ye be without chastisement, whereof all are partakers, then are ye bastards, and not sons." **Heb. 12:6-8.**

CHAPTER 3

WEEK THREE:

Developing Your Spiritual Weapons – "Don't Give Up"

DAY 15: Examine your spiritual self: Understand you are a sinner.

DAY 16: Develop a sincere desire for the Word of God.

DAY 17: Trust in the Lord to bring you out of your troubles.

DAY 18: Recognize and resist the devil's lies.

DAY 19: See your need for God.

DAY 20: Fast: Hunger and thirst not for food and drink but for God.

DAY 21: Do spiritual exercises.

The operative word here is "develop." You may be familiar with this word and have a good idea as to what it means, but do you fully understand the depth of its purpose? What I'd like to do here is to make sure the developmental stage will be well understood and taken very seriously, so that you will not be tricked into giving up. **Proverbs 4:5** says: "Get wisdom, get understanding: forget it not …." Understanding will bring you into great knowledge and comprehension for the journey you've become a part of. On this journey you will be encouraged, learn the statutes of God and seek to know Him more and more. "My people are destroyed for lack of knowledge," **Hosea 4:6.** "Develop," as defined in Wikipedia, is to "grow or cause to grow and become mature, advance or elaborate; also, having reached an advanced stage of mental or emotional development characteristic of an adult." In order to accomplish the task of growing or developing in the Lord as a Christian, you must examine yourself to make sure you understand you are a sinner, saved by the grace of God. There is not one iota of anything you can do to earn being a Christian, other than accepting Jesus Christ, as its stated in scripture. "That if thou shalt confess with thy mouth the Lord Jesus, and shalt believe in thine heart that God hath raised Him from the dead, thou shalt be saved." **(Rom. 10:9)** Every day there will be challenges. You must take responsibility for your own growth and development for living victoriously as a child of God. Listed are some personal steps I believe you must take to ensure a successful developmental process in remaining stable in the everlasting love of the Lord.

- You must have a sincere desire for the word. **1 Peter 1:2**

- Must desire to live it. **2 Cor. 5:15**
- Study it. **2 Tim. 2:15**
- Practice it. **Rom. 12:2**
- Defend it. **1 Pet. 3:15**
- Love the word **Jn. 14:15**

Now let's deal with "develop." Knowing specifically what you're developing is very important in growing closer to God. As **Ephesians 6:10-17** tells us, you must develop knowledge of the Word of God.

10. Finally, be strong in the Lord and the power of his might. 11. Put on the full armor of God so that you can stand the devil's schemes. 12. For our struggle is not against flesh and blood, but against the rulers, against the powers of this dark world and against the spiritual forces of evil in the heavenly realms. 13. Therefore put on the full armor of God, so that when the day of evil comes, you may be able to stand your ground, and after you have done everything, to stand. 14. Stand firm then, with the belt of truth buckled around your waist, with the breastplate of righteousness in place, 15. and with your feet fitted with the readiness that comes from the gospel of peace. 16. In addition to all this, take up the shield of faith, with which you can extinguish all the flaming arrows of the evil one. 17. Take the helmet of salvation and the sword of the spirit, which is the word of God.

Desire to Learn the Word of God

To desire the word of God, I always felt, is the first step to achieving a life in Christ. When you have within you a thirst and hunger, you will want to take every opportunity to be where you can receive and study the Word. You will know that you have the desire when you want to be where you can learn the Word, get to know God and let nothing prevent you from being where the Spirit of truth is in operation. When you have this desire, you will be fulfilling and doing what the Word says, "Put on the whole armor of God that you will be able to stand against the wiles of the devil." **(Eph. 6:11)** When the enemy brings strong forces against you, you will be confident knowing that you have great protection from him.

You will be enticed from many angles to return back by way of various temptations. God will allow you to be tempted. See the temptation comes from the devil; he waits for every opportunity, especially in your weakest moments, to attack you. But that's when God is allowing you to be tempted because there is no sin, he will not deliver you from. You're being tempted, but it's not sin until you yield or give in to it. God allows the devil to put you to the test. God wants your total allegiance. God withholds things you may desire, things you want or what you may need. Timing is God's specialty. You many have heard it said, "God is not a God of time but a God of timing." When you have a great need, that's when the devil makes you think you are in it all by yourself. Remember I said "think." Things may not be moving according to your thinking, and you begin to figure what you can do to fix or work out the situation. But this is when you should think "God is up to something on my behalf." Pray, seek and ask God what you should do. This is when you need to talk with someone, if the situation seems to be a bit overwhelming. Contact someone you know who can help you through the rough times of testing. Yes, testing. God is watching. "The eyes of the Lord are in every place, beholding evil and the good." **(Proverbs 15:3);** you will find out through your tests, if you trust Him. Usually most people say, "God wants to see if you trust Him," but I'd like you to know that God already knows what you will do. He wants you to see what you will do. You will soon learn whether you trust Him or trust what your own ingenuity can accomplish. This is when many backslide!

I will share with you this testimony. I have many. This one happened several years ago. I was facing retirement under some specific circumstances in which my resources were held up. I had very little income, compared to what I had originally. To add insult to injury, after waiting for a very long time, I received a letter and thought it would be the answer to the prayer I was expecting. To my surprise, it was disappointing news. My case could not be heard because the courts were backlogged. My bills were backlogged. My husband was holding it down best he could with one income, as opposed to two incomes. What I was helping with could no longer satisfy all we needed to meet the household bills. Pressure was building (bills) waiting for the Lord to answer. Finances became very tight for the both of us. We were being put to the test. We continued our fellowship with the church, praying, fasting and giving what we were obligated to give. The more I prayed, it seemed God was not hearing; things kept getting more difficult, even to the point I remember in prayer service I prostrated myself before the Lord and cried out to God. I had not shared this with anyone – it was between God and me. I wish I could tell you that I didn't have too much longer to wait, but I did. But I waited on the Lord. As the Psalmist David said, "I waited patiently for the Lord; he turned to me and heard my cry. He lifted me out of the slimy pit, out of the mud and mire; he set my feet on a rock and gave me a firm place to stand. **Ps. 40:1-2 (NIV).**

After a while, daylight had come, and weeping had ceased. That time period was a very trying experience; sometime later, a letter did come in the mail stating that due to the heavy load of court cases, my case would be heard in the basement of Holiday Inn. Well, the day came, and my case was heard, and there was no reason for them to deny what I had worked for; I was granted my request, and it was made retroactive. It was a difficult test, but we trusted God and He showed Himself faithful.

I could easily have found other means of borrowing, but for me there was no other way; in other words, I was "sold out" to waiting and trusting God. I trusted the Word "… weeping may remain for a night, but rejoicing comes in the morning." **Ps. 30:5 (NIV)** I trusted God before, and He brought me out, I knew He would bring me out again. "But those who hope in the Lord will renew their strength. They will soar on wings like eagles; they will run and not grow weary; they will walk and not be faint." **Is. 40:31 (NIV)** When you know what the Word says, you repeat it to yourself, and as you pray, you will gain strength within your spirit; you will begin to rehearse the Word. Then will you realize rejoicing will be necessary. I will admit, it was a great test – in my weakness, I cried out to God for help to continue to trust Him. In those weak moments, I didn't give up. I lay before God in prayer and fasting and reading His Word.

Your Mouth is a Powerful Weapon

Your mouth is your greatest weapon if you use it to say the Word of God. Do it positively with authority. I read a story when I was first saved about this farmer who for years had not had a good harvest. He kept saying, every year he didn't have a good crop, "I had a bad year last year and all the other years; I know this year will be the same way. I won't have a good year this year, either." Guess what? He didn't. Your words are very powerful. Use them to speak what you want to happen positively. You must speak to make what you want to happen. Words are POWERFUL!!!!

This may seem factitious, but the Bible emphatically declares in **Proverbs 18:21**, "Death and life are in the power of the tongue; and they that love it shall eat the fruit thereof." When you love the Word, you will use your tongue to bring forth the fruit (edible or useable) of what you want it to produce; you will love to speak good things or positive things, knowing it will produce the best for you and you will enjoy it. You will receive what you desire.

Praise is another powerful weapon the devil will try to keep you from using or doing. He will tell you LIES, to prevent you from wanting to praise God in church with other believers. Here are some things he does to achieve his mission, which is to steal, kill and destroy. Let's explore. Here are some common things he says to achieve his goal:

- It doesn't take all that ...
- You're crazy and you look crazy for doing that ...
- A person with your status or credentials doesn't act like that ...
- That's not how intelligent people behave ...
- You're a holy roller ...
- They are going to call you a Jesus only or a holy roller ...
- That's too much noise, people will think you're crazy ...
- You have to give too much money ...
- Speaking in tongues is not necessary – you don't have to speak in tongues...
- People of intelligence don't want to be a part of anything like that ...
- You don't have to go to church so much ...

Of course, he will tell you that you go to church too much, that you don't have to get that involved. All you have to do is get on an auxiliary, pay your tithes and give an offering – that's all you need to do – and just go when you feel like it. This will come from familiar sources (churchgoers). The point I'm making here is that the devil wants to keep you ignorant, because when you don't totally commit, you will not fulfill the plan God has for you; the more ignorant you are, the better he can keep you from being a threat to him and his mission. Yes, you are a threat to his mission, which is to steal, kill and destroy. Destroying you will leave one less person keeping his mission from being achieved. How he destroys is that by keeping you ignorant, he will place negative influences in your life to break down your ambition, which will more likely than not lead to destructive behavior. His plan is to prevent you from winning souls God has ordained for you to witness, which will bring them into the Saving Grace of Jesus Christ. The fruit of the righteous is a tree of life; and he that winneth souls is wise. **Prov. 11:30**

I am sure there are many, many more lies and half-truths he tells, I just want to share what he has told me and others I know. If he can kill your desire or steal it out of your heart, then and only then can he lead you away from God and the things of God. He will let you stay close enough to give you the illusion you are in the plan of God. Let me just say that he is not crazy, you are that important that he cares about you in that he wants to help you – remember he's a liar and he's God's archenemy. The Bible says, "The serpent was more subtle (cunning) than any beast of the field..." **Gen. 3:1.** It's important to study the Word. Always remember, "It's nice to be important, but it's much more important to be nice." I was taught this at a very young age by one of my elementary school teachers; the Bible teaches you to prefer another above oneself.

Many people think that giving to build the kingdom of God is a big rip-off. But when there is a death or tragedy in their families, they are some of the same ones who want — and expect — the Church to come to their rescue. If the church doesn't help, they will say very harsh and negative things, categorizing all churches; then angry attitudes develop toward the Church. What most people fail to understand is that it's the people in the building – not the building itself – whose faith and finances they are relying on to support what they, themselves, never bothered to support.

Enter Through the Narrow Gate

The Bible says, "The fear of the Lord is the beginning of wisdom." Seek God daily to "work out your own salvation with fear and trembling." **Phil. (2:12b)** But not without a pastor or overseer to give spiritual guidance. Again, this helps you to know the Word, which is a must, in order for you or anyone to gain understanding and grow spiritually. There are things that others may do that just may not be for you. Where they appear to be spiritual, they may not be there spiritually at all. So just seek God in prayer and stay under a Great Anointed Leader. God will show Himself strong in you.

Think about it: Before you came to Christ, you did what you felt you were big and bad enough to do or influenced to do. Basically, you may think, "I did what I wanted to do." But in all honesty, you did what your daddy, the devil, wanted you to and you loved it. Yes, your daddy! He's not going to give you bad thoughts about what you're doing apart from God's Word. When you were doing it, he was sending and putting things in your paths for you to continue doing it. He helps create more and more avenues for you to continue on that path. He does this because he wants to keep you blind. Why blindness? Simple, you won't see your future with him in Hell. Many have their connotation about hell. They say things like, "I'm catching Hell now"; I'm living in Hell"; "You create your own Hell"; "Hell is right here on Earth" – just to mention a few. The Hell the Bible speaks of is in no way near the things you will face here on Earth. Remember the song "On Broadway"? It says, "The lights are much brighter there, you can forget all your troubles forget all your cares." **Matt. 7:13 (NIV)** says, "Enter through the narrow gate. For wide is the gate and broad is the road that leads to destruction, and many enter through it." You can forget your troubles, but that doesn't mean they are forgotten or gone away for good. When the lights go out on Broadway, what are you going to do? You must go home. Your problems are still there. Your situation that took you there has not changed. Ignoring or sweeping problems under the rug, so-to-speak, has never rendered successful results.

I recall a situation that happened in Niagara Falls decades. ago called the Love Canal. What happened, after so many years of living there, people in the Love Canal area began showing obvious signs of illnesses. Reports started to surface of babies born deformed, mothers with health issues and so many other sicknesses. Research was done, and the problems were traced back to toxic chemicals dumped on that site years earlier, then covered up, with homes built on top of the toxic pollution there. You must understand, every situation has a remedy; it must be dealt with in a proper fashion. Hiding it will only delay sometimes the horrific consequences that can lead to destruction.

God is the only one who can give you help to deal with any situation you may have, when you give Him the opportunity.

You must see your need for God. He is the creator of the universe as well as your creator, who has all power in his hand. Letting God help is far better than trying to do it yourself – masking your troubles with a fake smile and achieving temporary joy without going through the proper procedure. Oh, you may make mistakes. But making a mistake or being tricked are not reasons to turn away from God, which is exactly what the devil wants you to do. That's exactly when you should turn to God. He wants to show you His loving kindness, tender mercy, compassion and every emotion needed to assure you it's all right. He loves you. If you were perfect, then you would have no need for God, because you would never make a mistake. It's the way to prove His word, Forgiveness.

Casting all your cares upon him for he careth for you. **1 Peter 5:7**

"If we confess, our sins, he is faithful and just to forgive us our sins, and to cleanse to us from all unrighteousness." **1 John 1:9**

"Come unto me, all ye that labour and are heavy laden, and I will give you rest. Take my yoke upon you, and learn of me, for I am meek and lowly in heart: and ye shall find rest unto your souls. For my yoke is easy, and my burden is light." **Matt. 11: 28 -30**

"My little children, these things write I unto you, that ye sin not. And if any man sin, we have an advocate with the Father, Jesus Christ the righteous." **1 John 2:1** What a loving and compassionate Father, whose concern for each and every one of His children is so genuine in that He knows each of us to provide for us. Every person who loves God, trusts Him and accepts Him as Lord and Savior can load all of their cares, all of their woes, all of their sorrows, every thought, on Him. He is sovereign, is able to shoulder every last one, put them all in perspective, to make you the salt of the earth **(Matt. 5:13),** HALLELUJAH! What the Bible says about Hell.

Please focus: Whether you, or anyone else for that matter, believes or doesn't believe there is a hell, it doesn't negate the fact that there is one. Let me share a truth with you. I was 36 years old had two lovely and handsome sons. Did I mention HANDSOME?!!! Anyway, I was 36, my boys were 12 and 10, and the Lord told me – yes, told me – I was going to have a daughter. He showed me the little girl, as I was on my knees at the altar in church service one Sunday morning. I became very concerned because I knew it was the Lord; but why, at 36, with two almost-teenage sons, was I being told about a daughter? Mind you, I desired a daughter during my two pregnancies, but not at 36. After affirming that God was really telling me I was going to have a daughter, my prayer was like that of Jesus in the Garden of Gethsemane: "Lord let this cup pass from me." I was not at the "nevertheless moment" – it took me a moment. Hey, sometimes it's just that way. Nevertheless, I did get there. After many conversations with the Lord, I realized God had spoken, and I was going to have to obey and have a daughter.

Of course, the conversation wasn't over. I said to God: "If I'm going to have a girl when I become pregnant, I don't want to be wishing and hoping it's a girl, I want to know for sure."

He said, "Just ask me." My response: "Okay Lord, that makes sense."

I said: "Well, when I ask you, I want to know for sure, beyond the shadow of doubt, that you said, yes."

He said: "Just ask me a yes-or-no question." I said: "Oh, that makes sense." So that night in prayer I asked the Lord,

"Can I have a girl?"

He said, "Yes." It was just that simple. I started to get up from my knees, I stopped and said, "Wait a minute Lord" then I said, "Oh, Lord what shall I name her?

The Lord said, "Cookie." Well, as the saying goes, the rest is history. She came in weighing 7lbs. ½ oz. There is a very important reason for me telling you this.

I must let you know that during my nine months, I met with many challenges from various individuals questioning me as if I had not heard from God. Also concerned ones thought they were looking out for my best interest because they thought I was carrying a boy from the looks of things. Some people think they have the gift of "just looking and can tell" what you are carrying. When I say I had many challenges, there's no mistake in words. I want you to know God is good … because when I had had enough of people's opinions and speculations, I consulted Abba (knowing He is my caring Father). Sitting in church service one Sunday morning where the aggravation was very heavy on my mind and communing with Him, He flipped my Bible open right as I sat in Church, His Word popped out at me from the pages in **Romans 3:3-4** "For what if some did not believe? Shall their unbelief make the faith of God without effect? God forbid: Yea, let God be true, but every man a liar ..." So, in other words, what people say about what they think, really doesn't matter. I said all of this to bring you to the point that what people say, about Hell and everything else about the Bible isn't important, but the Words written in it are important. What any and everyone need to be aware of is, and I repeat:

What they believe does not change the Word of God or make it of no effect.

Hell has enlarged herself, and opened her mouth without measure ..." **Is. 5:14**

"But the fearful, and unbelieving, and the abominable, and murderers, and whoremongers, and sorcerers, and idolaters, and all liars, shall have their part in the lake which burneth with fire and brimstone: which is the second death." **Rev. 21:8** "And in hell he lift up his eyes, being in torments, ..." **Lk. 16:23**

No matter what anyone thinks, if it doesn't line up with the Word of God, they are wrong. So many things concerning Bible prophecy have come to pass, and circumstances in the world are leading to more prophecies being fulfilled. If the Word of God were going to fail, it would have done so by now. If you were once with God and have backslid and/or you are feeling the tugging of the Lord on your heart, you need to continue reading this book. It's for you, a friend and others. Give them a copy as a gift.

"Trust in the Lord with all thine heart; and lean not unto thine own understanding." **Prov. 3:5**

For the past 30 years, I've seen people running from one place to the other trying to appease God through their own thinking, works and lusts. Saying things such as, "We should not judge – that's what the Bible says." And "God loves me."

"God doesn't care what I wear to Church." "God wants us to be happy." "God doesn't send anybody to hell." "It doesn't matter where I go to church, as long as I go." "As long as I do good to everyone." "I volunteer my services at the church and do mission work." Remember **Romans 3:3-4?** Here's something else the Bible says about it.

"That if thou shalt confess with thy mouth the Lord Jesus, and shalt believe in thine heart that God hath raised him from the dead, thou shalt be saved. **Rom 10:9.**

"Therefore, if any man be in Christ, he is a new creature:

old things are passed away; behold, all things are become new." **2 Cor. 5:17**. Openly confessing Jesus Christ is the first step to entering into the family of God, a personal relationship with God and assurance of Salvation. It is definitely through his Son, the Lord Jesus Christ. Understanding and believe: "For God so loved the world, that he gave his only begotten Son, that whosoever believeth in him shall not perish, but have everlasting life." **John 3:16.** This starts a loving relationship such as none other you will ever know.

Come As You Are, But Come

When I was first regenerated, times were very different than they are now. There were many rules in the church. Like the dress code – oh, a biggie at some churches and may still be at a few. Women had to wear dresses or skirts, which had to be a certain length below the knees; no sleeveless tops were allowed, no bare legs, no makeup, no large earrings – and the list goes on. But what you wear to church, to a certain degree, shouldn't matter, as long as it's not too outrageous, I suppose. (Let me preface this by saying when you get God in you, you'll know how to present yourself). But most importantly, when going to the house of the Lord wanting to be saved, how to do it victoriously should be the first and foremost matter at hand. Clothing should not hinder you or anyone from going into the house of the Lord to get instructions for the soul. Come as you are but come!

But many years ago, a dress code was just a part of the teaching. My first Pastor, my dad (yeah, I was a PK – a preacher's kid) ascribed to that teaching (It was the way it was then). Many of the more seasoned (older) saints, when I rededicated my life to the Lord some years later, still had the same mentality. **Romans 14:21** says: "It is good neither to eat flesh, nor to drink wine, nor any thing whereby thy brother stumbleth, or is offended, or is made weak." A dress code, for example, could be their way of helping churchgoers stay on the straight and narrow. If what you wear offends when you come into the knowledge of God, then it's inappropriate. In my day, they didn't wait, they just told you. It was like a church fashion emergency, and they had to take care of immediately. "Houston, we have a problem." Well, I just wanted to be saved, so whatever it took, whatever the rule, I accepted it. That bird doesn't fly too much anymore; every individual's heart should determine what's appropriate and what's not, according to the Word of God.

The Word of God teaches that if something you're doing offends someone, then show love; don't do it while in their presence. For some people, this is an issue. But to God, it really isn't: He already knows your path. The Holy Spirit will lead and guide you into what's right and away from what's wrong. It's your responsibility or your love for Him to remain dedicated to the relationship by reading and studying His Word. Spiritually, do you think what you wear to church is the real issue God is most concerned about? The Word does say "everything in moderation."

Too often, too much focus is put on the outside and not enough on the real issue: the inside (the inward man). Your soul – the seat of your affections, emotions and desires – will cause you to lose focus. It looks for those things that draw attention to the body, so that when others see it they can lavish it with praise; it makes you feel good, and your soul seeks more and more. This is the biggest area in which Satan can defeat any and everyone; seeking to please the flesh.

"This I say then, walk in the Spirit and ye shall not fulfill the lust of the flesh." **Gal. 5:16**

The help that's needed to defeat the self-seeking, self-motivation fleshly lust is the Word, Prayer and Fellowship with other believers. Having fellowship with mature believers will encourage you to seek the will of God.

"Set your affection on things above, not on things on this earth." **Col. 3:2**

How do you set your affection on things above I am so glad you ask. You must be determined to focus on what's important and what's not. You must not kid yourself. It's going to take loving devotion towards God, as the scripture says, "Thou shalt love the Lord thy God with all thy heart, and with all thy soul, and with all thy mind." **Matt. 22:37.** I've found out it's really not hard to do if you really have a made-up mind and you want to do the will of God. In the world, you develop habits. You're taught or influenced by a lot of negative things; even being a witness to wrong things, you can become influenced. Some are embedded so deeply that you don't always know they are there or that there is anything wrong with what you do or say. It's necessary for me to say, being in love with the Word doesn't mean you can't have a life full of joy. You can enjoy other things in life – movies, bowling, karaoke, parks – the list is endless. Just don't forget about God and what pleases Him.

God doesn't want your affection to be set on the things of the world, but rather by His Word. "As newborn babes, desire the sincere milk of the word, that ye may grow thereby," **(1 Peter 2:2.)** You must sincerely desire to know the Lord. His Word is the first place to start. It is at this point a "heart transplant" can easily take place to reveal all of what's really in the heart. Therefore, you can pray and seek God for cleansing, like David, having your heart renewed with affection toward God and the Word.

Fasting makes the body/flesh behave This is a good place to talk about fasting, because it is another way of helping to cleanse you and redirect you to God's will.

This is a necessary act. This act of worship makes you aware that your body does not want to succumb to the obedience of God's word.

"... Be ye holy; for I am holy." **1 Peter 1:16.**

"Fasting is to position you for what God wants to do in your life!"

— Pastor Rod Parsley
World Harvest Church
Columbus, Ohio

Fasting helps clear the mind and forces you to seek God's help in defeating the temptations that will arise as obstacles to doing His will. It will take constant deliberate efforts to read, meditate, to sing songs of praise and prayer to overcome the urges to eat.

Fasting is preparation. You must prepare for any and everything that's important to you. If you think about it, that's exactly what you do for just about everything in your life you want to accomplish. Why should being a part of God's Army be any? As I said in Chapter 1, whatever is important, you will take time to protect it and secure it.

I'm going to share with some wisdom on fasting from a

pastor and author whose book I happened to pick up in Atlanta.

What happened, while my husband and I were visiting our sons, our eldest son knew we wanted to attend church service. He told his friend, whom he had visited with before, that he was bringing us to church. So, the young man reserved seats for us. We arrived and the Worship Team was singing, and the presence of the Lord filled the place. A few moments later, the pastor came out. It was, to my surprise, Pastor Jentezen Franklin, who is Senior Pastor of Free Chapel in Gainesville, Ga.

I was very familiar with him from TV. It was good to be at his church to hear him preach in person. Let me tell you, we were not disappointed either; his message was "Abraham's Last Test" — very timely and rewarding. I was excited my son enjoyed the message, too. We left with the Testimony it was good to have been there.

In the store, I saw his book on fasting and decided to buy it. I've always fasted from the very first time I dedicated my life to Christ and still do – not because I wanted to, but God wanted me to, and I felt He compelled me. So, after seeing Franklin's book, "Fasting," I purchased it with the intentions of using it, as a tool to teach from a seasoned pastor's perspective. Especially since I had done it all my saved life. I wanted to be obedient to God, because I've learned, "Obedience is better than sacrifice."

Here's what Jentezen Franklin has to say in "Fasting":

"What is fasting? Since there are so many misconceptions

about it, I first want to clarify what fasting – biblical fasting – is not. Fasting is not merely going without food for a period of time. That is dieting – maybe even starving – but fasting it is not. Nor is fasting something done only by fanatics. I really want to drive this home. Fasting is not to be done only by religious monks alone in a cave somewhere. The practice of fasting is not limited to ministers or to special occasions.

Stated simply, biblical fasting is refraining from food for spiritual purpose. Fasting has always been a normal part of a relationship with God. As expressed by the impassioned plea of David in Psalm 42, fasting brings one into a deeper, more intimate and powerful relationship with the Lord.

When you eliminate food from your diet for a number of days, your spirit becomes uncluttered by things of the world and amazingly sensitive to the things of God. Amen! (This is my feeling). As David stated, "Deep calls unto the deep." (Ps. 42:7). David was fasting. His hunger and thirst for God were greater than his natural desire for food. As a result, he reached a place where he could cry out from the depths of his spirit to the depths of God, even in the midst of his trial. Once you've experienced even a glimpse of that kind of intimacy with our God – our Father, the holy creator of the universe – and the countless rewards and blessings that follow, your whole perspective will change. You will realize that fasting is a secret source of power that is overlooked by many.

A threefold cord is not quickly broken. — **Ecclesiastes 4:12**

During the years that Jesus walked this earth, He devoted

time to teaching His disciples – the principles of the Kingdom of God–principles that conflict with those of this world. In the Beatitudes, specifically in Matthew 6, Jesus provided the pattern by which each of us is to live as a child of God. That pattern addressed three specific duties of a Christian: giving, praying, and fasting. Jesus said, "When you give…" and "When you pray…" and "When you fast." He made it clear that fasting, like giving and praying, was a normal part of Christian life. As much attention should be given to fasting as is given to giving and to praying."

Every time I fasted; I always felt a great effect from it – spiritually understanding the natural. You've got to know the importance of fasting – how it really allows God's Spirit to minister to you on a level that leaves you with and brings you into a deeper maturity and understanding of self and others – biblically and naturally. From the first time I was told to fast, I've fasted to this day. There has not been one week in which I did not take a day to fast – from 1976 to this year. It helps put things in perspective for the child of God. I can't stress enough to you how important this part of your growth and development this is. Fasting brings you to a place that you can see who you really are.

David understood. Take a look at the following scriptural passages:

"Have mercy on me, O God, according to your unfailing love; according to your great compassion blot out my transgression. 2. Wash away all my iniquity and cleanse me from my sin. 3. For I know my transgression, and my sin is always before me. 4. Against you, you only have I sinned and done what is evil in your sight, so that you are proved right when you speak and justified when you judge. Surely, I was sinful at birth, sinful from the time my mother conceived me." **Psalm 51:1-5. (NIV)**

Cleanse me with hyssop, and I will be clean; wash me, and I will be whiter than snow. **Psalm. 51:7(NIV)**

10. Create in me a pure heart, O God and renew a steadfast spirit within me. **Ps. 51:10 (NIV)**

The Word will be a mirror. It will help you see things in you that are not Christ-like, things you do, as well as the way you think. As you are cleansed through fasting, it allows a pathway for your affection to be saturated in the praise and glory of God, through the Word and fellowship. Your affection will be turned towards God. The spirit of a new

babe takes place in the Lord. Like a newly born baby – very supple in the hands of its mother – so are you in the hands of a mature Spirit-filled man or woman of God in a (heal) thy environment, where the training of a WARRIOR can take place. Take note that "heal" is in parentheses: It is there purposely to let you know every person may not be well or healed. Sometimes they appear to be healed. They come from various walks of life and/or different churches where they have been hurt, misused or insulted and they cover it up.

They put on a garment of strength and steadfastness so they will give the illusion that they have it all together. But the moment things go differently from their expectation, a door opens, and their hidden pain is revealed. You – as a new babe in Christ or a returning convert – must be aware of this situation so that you are not pulled into a web of unresolved issues, which starts a wave of negative thoughts, problems and disillusionments. This may have been a problem for some who found themselves in a backslidden state. That's why I felt led to write this book, so no one can fall prey to this tactic of Satan again. He wants to fulfill his mission, "To steal, kill and destroy," **John 10:10.**

Boot Camp–Spiritual Discipline

If you were to talk with someone who served time in any branch of the military, they would tell you the first thing they had to do is go to Boot Camp, and it's no walk in the park by any stretch of the imagination. I can recall when my brother served in the Vietnam War, we wrote to each other quite frequently from the time he was sent away until he returned home. My harsh reality came when he wrote me telling me about the harsh treatment, he, along with other enlistees, received in boot camp. The drills were repeated until some nearly passed out, with platoon leaders up in their faces, yelling, showing no respect, despite the weather, cold or hot, sunshine or rain, nasty and dirty.

If you've ever been treated badly, multiply it by any umber, and that's boot camp. It is harsh and cruel treatment and seeing it on TV doesn't begin to describe the reality of it. But there's a purpose for it all! It all has to do with conditioning for battle.

There's a spiritual boot camp, which is designed to condition you for battle as well. I wish I could tell you there isn't, but – reality check – there is! This is why I want to help prepare you to be armed and dangerous against the enemy.

When the devil sees you and easily identifies you as a child of God, he will become afraid. You are one who was in God's presence after accepting Him as Lord and Savior; ready for battle, a force to be reckoned with. You have tough skin, spiritually. When you make Jesus your Lord and Savior, you have declared:

1. You are no longer your own, you have given lordship over to Jesus Christ.

2. You've declared that He is the resurrected Son of God

3. You're under the bloodstained banner of the Lord, washed in His Blood. David, in **1 Sam. 17**, saw the giant, Goliath, as the enemy to Israel. Just as there were enemies to the children of God in Biblical times, there still are today – nothing has changed. You must recognize the same enemy is against you.

The enemy may not come as a giant, 9 or more feet in height, and challenge you physically, but he will come in different forms that can affect you mentally. David saw the chance to cause a change to take place and he accepted the challenge. There are times when you will have to accept the challenge, when forced into "valley experiences," just understand as Pastor Parsley taught us – that the valley is where God brought you for your enemy to die. Those valleys are there to bring about changes. Will you take the challenges God allows to confront you? Then, and only then, as a new creation and as a believer in Christ, the Word will show forth in your life.

When you face difficult challenges or feel you are losing control of your life, trust in God and allow Him to lead and guide, as He so desires, to bring about the change that's needed in you. As you continue surrendering your will, you'll see within you a new creature emerging in thoughts and behavior. The way God does things will not be the way you or anyone thinks He will do it or even the way you would like Him to handle the situation. But recognize that God is in control, working things out for your good.

"And we know that all things work together for good to them that love God, to them who are the called according to his purpose." **Romans 8:28.**

Do your spiritual exercise, pray, sing songs of praise, worship, meditate and talk about His goodness by maintaining healthy relationships – until your change comes. I am reminded of babies when they become aware of their ability to walk alone; they reject help or the touch of anyone, but they still need assistance. In the same way, you, a newborn babe in Christ, may feel you can walk independently, be among people you hung with prior to your conversion and can handle their walk and their talk. But it's not true – you still need help – and separation from negative influences! I pray along with your prayer that this book will be a great help to you. David, in **1 Samuel 17:26**, was up for a challenge. He said, "... Who is this uncircumcised Philistine, that he should defy the armies of the living God?" Saul gave David his armor. David refused it. He had no experience with that type of weaponry. So, as it is with you, a new convert when it comes to defeating the devil. You need assistance.

The Bible is your ultimate weapon. This book is a Bible-based weapon that you can handle until you get the strength you need to defeat the devil. Then you will be ready to take him on, along with his cohorts through the power of the Holy Spirit and the Word. It deals with the sincere milk of the Word. In other words, a "right now" Word. Something you can easily handle and understand. As long as a person can read or have someone else read it to them, this weapon is a powerful tool in your hand as well as in their hand; it can and will help you defeat the devil. Then, you won't want to backslide or even think about backsliding. You will understand the dangers you will face. It also unfolds the price paid by Jesus Christ.

If they fall away, to be bought back to repentance, because to their loss they are crucifying the Son of God all over again and subjecting Him to public disgrace. **Heb. 6:6 (NIV)**

Of them (the unrighteous) the Proverbs are true: "A dog returns to its vomit," and "A sow that is washed goes back to her wallowing in the mud." **2 Pet. 2:22 (NIV)**

If you don't stay committed to your acknowledgement, acceptance and confession of Jesus Christ as your Savior; you will return to familiar behaviors. As the Scripture says, returning to those things you partook of prior to your regeneration, not living according to His statutes, you return to your former sinful image and lifestyle. Living as if Christ has never done anything for you. Jesus is right back on the cross of suffering all over again.

He will take your stony heart and give you a heart of flesh **(Ezek. 11:19).** If you continue the study of His Word, continue in fellowship with the saints, prayer and fasting this will prevent you or anyone from backsliding. Only God knows the heart **(Jer. 17:9).** His Word and your prayers are the powerful force that will give you the strength to stay on the straight and narrow. The heart is deceitfully and desperately wicked **(Jer. 17:9).** It takes God to cleanse it from ungodly thoughts and actions. To give you the kind of love only He can give. To love God is to love His Word. He is the Word manifested in the flesh **(John 1:14).**

Loving God obediently will change your heart, prepare you for the Heavenly Kingdom and grant you blessings designed specifically for you as you grow and live for Him. Also, it causes you to see things differently – the way God wants you to see them. He hung, bled and died on Calvary for your sins.

CHAPTER 4

WEEK FOUR:

Staying Connected – Relationship, Fellowship & Worship

DAY 22: Build a relationship with God through communication, prayer.

DAY 23: Build fellowship with like-minded believers

DAY 24: Worship and pray as if your spiritual life depended on it (It does!)

DAY 25: Become God's vessel – keep your spiritual ears open.

DAY 26: Know the devil's roadblocks so you can avoid them.

DAY 27: Establish a regular prayer life.

DAY 28: Hang in there with God and discover his plan for you.

Every relationship starts with some type of connection or/and communication. That connection can be physical attraction, a simple liking for the same things, such as a certain song or movie, sports, or the outdoors. It's no different when it comes to making a connection with your Heavenly Father. The moment you first become interested in the Lord, that's the moment when He touched you and brought your attention to Him. It's His intention to develop your spirit to connect with Him. In other words, He wants to develop a relationship with you, and you with Him.

Can you remember the exact moment when you met that special person that you wanted to get to know? Do you recall the feeling that went over you and how you felt? You wanted very much to meet and spend time with him or her. You made it happen. Nothing and no one could get in your way. I don't want you to focus on how it ended, if it has (That memory will prove important later), but don't go there yet. Remain focused on the initial feeling! As Paul wrote in **Philippians 4:8** "Finally, brothers (sisters) whatever is true, whatever is noble, whatever is right, whatever is pure, whatever is lovely, whatever is admirable – if anything is excellent or praiseworthy – think about such things." Every relationship starts off in a certain mode, such as, "I can't get enough of you" – that type of feeling. It's a beautiful thing.

When Christ touches your heart, it's somewhat the same kind of experience – jubilance. The only difference is that He's not someone you can see or touch physically. But you can be touched and touch Him in the innermost parts of your being – your spirit. The way it's done is through His Word,

the one who kicked him (Satan) out of Heaven – he's going to harass you with everything he possibly can. Heaven is a place that he knows exists, because he was there. He can't ever go back. Therefore, he's trying to rally as many as he can to take to Hell with him, and two-thirds of the heavenly host he took, when he was kicked out, in order to get back at God. All I can say, don't be a part of his revenge. God has greater and better things in store for you. A couple of scriptures I want to mention right here that are very clear about Hell.

In **Matt. 25:41**: "Depart from me, ye cursed, into everlasting fire, prepared for the devil and his angels:"

And in **Rom. 12:19**: "... Vengeance is mine; I will repay, saith the Lord."

Hell was not made for humankind. It's imperative to develop a loving relationship with your Savior. As you relate in the natural, so it is in the spiritual, first. If the thought hasn't popped in your mind that you should have a loving relationship with Christ, it's okay, because now, in this book you're reading, I'm prompting you to establish one. The loving relationship you develop will be the lifeline to your victory. If you live without Christ Jesus, there is no way you can survive victoriously. It is vital that you have a personal relationship with the Father through Jesus Christ the righteous.

In the beginning of any relationship, communication must take place. To continue the analogy of a boyfriend / girlfriend relationship, spending time together is the avenue that causes understanding to develop. You need to learn things about

71

each other to see if there is compatibility. During the process, you each will learn the likes and dislikes, interests, and hopes for the future. Again, so it is with Christ. You discover as you, pray, read, fellowship, worship and praise God. You learn about and appreciate Him. You learn what He sacrificed for you, and He reveals things about yourself.

FELLOWSHIP

Another "ship" that has to be considered is Fellowship – a very big part of the relationship. As the saying goes, "No man is an island." When you are around others, character-building takes place; it's revealed, nurtured and developed. Others sometimes have the ability to bring things out of you that you may not have known were there. If you are single, you will likely become involved with someone as a potential mate. You will definitely want to fellowship with others who will help you emotionally to remain focused spiritually. Let's face it, LOVE is sometimes blind. Love allows you to see the good in a person or what the person wants you to see.

God never hurts. God is Love. But situations, when entered into without serious consideration in prayer, may cause you to be hurt. Dealing with personalities will uncover behaviors in a potential mate that may cause you to take a second look, see things differently. You may not be able to deal with it. Therefore, this will give you an opportunity to seek advice from a seasoned, mature saint to see if it's something that needs to be addressed professionally or spiritually, or if you want to be in relationship with that person at all. Let me dispel this myth before I go any further: Just because you are saved and the person, you're interested in is saved, doesn't mean you're good for one another. All this means is that you are worshipping the same God, or you believe in the same God. Fellowship is good in revealing true character. Some people can be cancerous to you or stifling to your relationship with God. It takes fellowship to reveal the good the bad and the ugly. Your fellowship with God will help you to see yourself for who you are. Fellowship forces you to see beyond the outer shell. When you listen to what a person says as they grow and testify, that's when the heart is revealed.

Your sincere commitment to God, to let Him make you to be the best you can be, will allow you to see the truth about yourself and help you totally surrender to Him. He can cleanse you and make you the new creation His word promises to do.

"Any man in Christ is a new creation, old things are passed away and behold all things are made new." **2 Cor. 5:17**

Remember fellowshipping with other like-minded believers is always necessary. Why? Because you gain strength. The enemy of your soul knows this, and he knows if he can keep you away, he can conquer. It's like that very familiar saying, "Divide and conquer." It's a very successful strategy the enemy knows works, this way he can accomplish his goal. Knowing it is half the battle. Knowledge is powerful. "And if one prevails against him, two shall withstand him; and a threefold cord is not easily broken." - **Ecc. 4:12**

WORSHIP

Last but not least is Worship, the third one of the "ships." Worship is very important, as well as fellowship and relationship. In my experience, "worship" is acknowledging the fact that God is Creator and there's none like Him. Understanding, giving Him reverence above all else. Knowing He is whom He says He is – written in His Word, the Bible.

There are many ways people may show their reverence to God. One thing we should always remember, as found in scripture, "But the hour cometh, and now is, when the true worshippers shall worship the Father in spirit and in truth; for the Father seeketh such to worship Him. God is a Spirit: and they that worship Him must worship Him in spirit and in truth." **John 4:23-24.**

What this means is: You've confessed Jesus as Lord, Savior; you truly believe Jesus is the Son of God, He is the Messiah; He's the living Redeemer of man's soul; and He is the Written Word. I'm sure there are other interpretations, but I believe knowing these facts, you can worship in spirit and in truth. I will include a short insight I found on the Internet, at **raptureready.com**, about worship. It starts with the question:

WHAT IS WORSHIP?

"Commonly, worship is considered to be the singing and praise part of a church service. While that is part of it, worship is truly so much more than that. God is not interested in rote forms of worship; He is interested in a heart that cries out to glorify Him. True worship is a life that honors Him.

Man and woman were created to worship God and even the hosts of Heaven worship Him.

I will point out some Scriptures that show how God has designed us to worship Him. We are to proclaim the Word of God **(1 Tim. 4:13)**. We are to respond gratefully to the truth of God **(Ex. 24:3)**. We are to remember the Lord's sacrifice through the celebration of communion **(1 Cor. 11:24, Acts 2:46 -47)**. We are to live godly lives **(1 Cor. 11:2)**. We are to sing psalms, hymns, and spiritual songs (Eph. 5:19). We are to pray in the Spirit **(Eph. 6:18)**. We are to present our entire selves to God **(Rom. 12:1)**. We are to offer a sacrifice of praise **(Heb. 13:15)**. We are to confess the name of God **(13:15)**. We are to do good things **(Heb. 13:16)**. We are to be generous and share with others **(Heb. 13:16)**.

These verses simply name a few of the ways in which we are to worship God. God is worthy of all of our praise. You can begin to read the Psalms to remind yourself of who God really is and why He deserves your praise."

(http://www.raptureready.com/)

Staying connected isn't just for you and you alone. You are God's vessel, bought with the precious blood of Jesus Christ. As a vessel dedicated to God, it is for the Lord. In the book of Jeremiah, Chapter 18, is a perfect example of how God wants to use us as His vessel. The Word goes on to say, "Then I went down to the potter's house, and behold, he wrought a work on the wheels. And the vessel that he made of clay was marred in the hand of the potter: so, he made it again another vessel, as seemed good to the potter to make it. Then the word of Lord came to me, saying, ... cannot I do with you as this potter? saith the Lord. Behold, as the clay is in the potter's hand, so are ye in mine hand ...." It is He, God, who wants to use you, to lead and guide you for His glory and honor, to reach souls to enlarge His kingdom. His assignments are for each of us to be His hands and feet. The word found in **2 Peter 3:9** declares this, "The Lord is not slack concerning His promise, as some men count slackness; but is longsuffering to us-ward, not willing that any should perish, but all should come to repentance."

Even though God wants everyone to be saved, in reality it's not going to happen, simply because there are many who will not believe in Him. Living a life for Christ will improve your personal life when you do things He requires. As I've mentioned earlier, studying the Word of God gives everything needed to live a victorious life as a child of God.

A Sense of Purpose

When God leads you, you really don't always know you are being led to fulfill a purpose. One thing for sure when you are doing that which is right, you don't have to wonder about it, you will be happy doing the right thing. I can recall the time when I felt in my heart to go to the Main Place Mall in downtown Buffalo. I'm mentioning this time in particular because I recall going to the mall with nothing specific in mind – just felt led to go. It wasn't until sometime later that the person that I spoke with while leaving the mall told me that what I said changed his life. Here's how it happened.

Early one afternoon it was in my heart to go to the mall. So, I got dressed and went. After arriving at the mall, I looked around and decided I had seen enough, since I didn't have anything in particular in mind that I needed. So, I decided to return home. As I was going down the stairs to exit the mall, I said hello to a young man I knew from college and he was also a very close friend of my brother, Gerald. We exchanged pleasantries. Then as we departed, I said to him something to the effect, "Good seeing you and whatever you do, keep your spiritual ears open." At this time, I didn't know I was being led by the Lord. I didn't know that I was on an assignment until years later. This will forever be etched in my mind.

At that time, I was a stay-at-home mom raising my sons. Some years later, I met up again with this mature gentleman, as he always was. We talked. It was great seeing him again. He said to me, "Sister Blanche, remember that day you saw me in the mall." I said "Yes." He said, "I wasn't living for the Lord as I should have, but after that day in the mall, it changed my life." He repeated, "What you told me that day in the mall really changed my life." I thank God that gentleman, Minister Chip Banks, is ministering the Gospel of Jesus Christ. We never know how God wants to use us; we just need to be a willing participant in this glorious Gospel of Jesus Christ. There are many occasions I can recall, but I believe you understand the point about being a vessel for God. Being led and being a servant of God, we don't always know, but it's always important to know God is depending on us to be ready to go as we are led. "For as many as are led by the Spirit of God, they are the Sons of God." Rom

8:14. As time went by, I've seen how God does, "... work all things together for good for those who love Him." **Rom. 8:28**

I'll list a few topics the devil, your adversary, the enemy of your soul, will have you do, to prevent you from entering into the level of depths and heights God wants you to come into.

The enemy will have you reject these simple situations, in that he can have you operate on a level you are familiar with, which is your own thinking and ways of doing things according to the flesh. In this way he is detaining or diverting you from real truth, the treasures found in the Word of God. Putting it simply: You will backslide if you let Satan have his way. He knows that God has great plans and wonderful things in store for you, for everyone who takes on the name of Jesus.

The word emphatically declares in Ephesians, Chapter 1 verses 4 and 5:

"According as he hath chosen us in him before the foundation of the world, that we should be holy and without blame before him in love."

The only way you can do this you must learn from His Word, what, is expected of you.

Also: "Having predestinated us unto the adoption of children by Jesus Christ to himself, according to the good pleasure of his will."

Here are a few things the devil tries to tell you:

1.) "Keep hanging with old friends – it's alright."

"Be ye not unequally yoked together with unbelievers: for what fellowship hath righteousness with unrighteousness? And what communion hath light with darkness? And what concord hath Christ with Belial? Or what part hath he that believeth with an infidel? And what agreement hath the temple of God with idols? For ye are the temple of the living God; as God hath said, I will dwell in them, and walk in them; and they shall be my people. Wherefore come out from among them, and be ye separate, saith the Lord, and touch not the unclean thing; and I will receive you.

And will be a Father unto you, and ye shall be my sons and daughters, saith the Lord Almighty." **2 Corinthians 6:14-18**

Anyone swimming in a pool is bound to get wet. It doesn't take a rocket scientist to figure that out. It's the same thing hanging with familiarity. Hanging with old friends, you will get involved with the same old things you indulged in before accepting Christ – and you will get wet. There is no such thing as hanging with them to win them for Christ. Even the strongest of Christians gets caught in that trap and backslides. There's a saying that goes like this: "If you play with fire, you will get burned." What God has delivered you from, He wants you to remain delivered. To continue the same old path is a sure way to backslide, returning to the things God delivered you from or wants to deliver you from.

You must be a willing participant. The Word says this: "Be not deceived: evil communications corrupt good manners." **1 Cor. 15:33**. In other words, when you continue hanging with those who have not accepted Christ as Savior, are not willing to trust God and obey His way of life, they will eventually convince you are missing out on having fun and whole a lot more. What they are essentially saying is, you are missing out on sinning; but ultimately, if you follow their lead, you're missing out on salvation ... Heaven.

2.) "Make excuses for not attending regular scheduled church affairs."

"Not forsaking the assembling of ourselves together, as the manner of some is but exhorting one another: and so much the more, as ye see the day approaching." — **Hebrews 10:25**

"That their hearts might be comforted, being knit together in love, and unto all riches of the full assurance of understanding, to the acknowledgement of the mystery of God, and of the Father, and of Christ; In whom are hid all the treasures of wisdom and knowledge. And this I say, lest any man should beguile you with enticing words." — **Colossians 2:2-4**

3.) "Don't Read God's Word"

"My people are destroyed for lack of knowledge: because thou hast rejected knowledge, I will also reject thee, that thou shall be no priest to me seeing thou hast forgotten the law of thy God, I will also forget thy children." **Hosea 4:6** "Beloved, think it not strange concerning the fiery trial, which is to try you, as though some strange thing happened unto you." **1 Peter 4:12**

There many tricks the devil will use to prevent you from becoming all God will have you accomplish. Of course, I did not mention how He will do everything humanly possible to

as though some strange thing is happening to you. Again, I remind you about what Apostle Peter says: "Beloved, think it not strange concerning the fiery trial, which is to try you, as though some strange thing happened unto you. But rejoice, inasmuch ye are partakers of Christ's sufferings." **1 Peter 4:12-13b.**

Oppositions are creatively designed by God to help develop and mature you. But the devil tries to use them against you, to impede growth. He wants to confuse you,

speaking lies to deter you from developing a close, personal relationship with the Lord. The devil knows that when you do, you can understand and will defeat him. It's all a test to prevent us from advancing to the levels God has already ordained to take us to, as we wait faithfully for His return.

The dictionary defines "test" as "a procedure intended to establish the quality, performance, or reliability of something." You are precisely the "something," the person God intends to establish for His glory. In establishing you, God will have to allow people, situations and spirit-filled leaders to teach you through trials and tests and His Word to build up your trust in Him. So, when the tests of life and circumstances come, you will not believe the lies of the devil, faint or give up. When you come through the trials and tests, your testimony will speak for itself. Let me encourage you: If you feel defeated in some of your tests or trials, persevere. Stay in the fight. "My little children, these things write I unto you, that ye sin not. And if any man (woman) sin, we have an Advocate with the Father, Jesus Christ the righteous." **1 John 2:1.**

The time will come for you as a born-again believer to take a stand, testify or help someone else. "But sanctify the Lord God in your hearts: and be ready always to give an answer to every man that asketh you a reason of the hope that is in you with meekness and fear ..." **1 Peter 3:15.** The Spirit of Truth will declare it through you and others will be touched and moved knowing you are a reliable source or a child of God.

Some people in the body of Christ will not come across to you in a way you may like. They may anger you or rub you the wrong way, so to speak. Remember the buffering I talked about earlier? Well, this is what I'm talking about. But not to worry, it's all a part of the test. When I talk about God allowing people to make you, this is how it's done.

I'll share with you what the Lord said to me one morning in prayer some years ago, long before I began to pastor. "You need each other to make each other." Also remember, our experiences are not only for ourselves, but for the body of Christ.

"Iron sharpeneth iron; so, a man sharpeneth the countenance of his friend." Prov. 27:17. I can recall when my son, Sharif, was about 16. He, his brother, Jamal, and sister, Cookie, all said good night and went upstairs to go to bed. A little while later, thinking they were all asleep, he came downstairs to my room and asked, "Mom, did you call me?" I said, "No, I didn't."

He said, "Oh, you're sure." My response was something to the effect, "I'm sure." He returned to his room upstairs. A few moments later he came back downstairs to me a second time and asked "Mom, you're sure you didn't call me?" Of course, I hadn't. This was his second trip downstairs to ask me if I had called him. So, immediately the story of Samuel and Eli came to my mind, and I realized what was happening. In 1 Samuel, third chapter, Samuel asked Eli a similar question. I told my son what Eli told Samuel. "If you hear it again, say speak Lord, I hear you."

"That the Lord called Samuel: and he answered, here am I. And he ran unto Eli and said Here am I; for thou calledst me. And he said, I called not; lie down again. And he went and lay down. And the Lord called yet again, Samuel, and Samuel arose and went to Eli, and said, here am I; for thou didst call me. And he answered, I called not, my son; lie down. Now Samuel did not yet know the Lord, neither was the word of the Lord yet revealed to him. And the Lord called Samuel a third time. And he arose and went to Eli, and said, here am I; for thou didst call me. And Eli perceived that the Lord had called the child." **1 Sam. 3:4-8.**

I mention this to encourage you to stay faithful to God. You don't know when or who will come to you needing an answer. Praying, fasting and giving unto the Lord are essentials (threefold cord) for every child of God. He will speak to you, giving you a Word when needed. If you worship, you will always be in relationship and fellowship with Him. "Patience" is key, in this process. There's a saying, "Haste makes waste." Or "Rome wasn't built in a day." It's all true!

"Make sure that your endurance carries you all the way without failing, so that you may be perfect and complete, lacking nothing." James 1:4 (Good News Bible) God wants to protect and provide for you and me, first and foremost; that's why He has given us His promises found in His Word.

"Trust in the Lord with all thine heart: and lean not unto thine own understanding. In all thy ways acknowledge Him, and He shall direct thy paths." Prov. 3:5, 6

The following insights are Red Flags I want to share with you in hopes of giving you a guideline to help you to determine if you are in danger of turning away, ready to walk away from the presence of God or Backslide!

7 Red Flags

1. You lack interest in reading the Word and other things of God you were once excited about. **Prov. 14:12; Rom. 4:21.**

2. You are comfortable being with those who have no interest in being a part of the family of God. **1 Cor. 1:18; 1 Cor. 15:33; Phil. 3;13-14.**

3. You complain about the songs sung, how the service is run and everything that takes place in the church. **Rom. 3:23; Gal. 6:1-10**

4. You make up excuses for not being able to attend Prayer and Bible Study or participating in other church activities. **Heb. 10:35, 36 and 38; Rom. 1:20-23**

5. You begin referring to the way you feel and how you feel it should go, wanting to disconnect. **John 15:4; Heb. 4:14-15**

Milton Keynes UK
Ingram Content Group UK Ltd.
UKHW020647201123
432908UK00019B/2479